Trading
Spaces

Instant
Impact

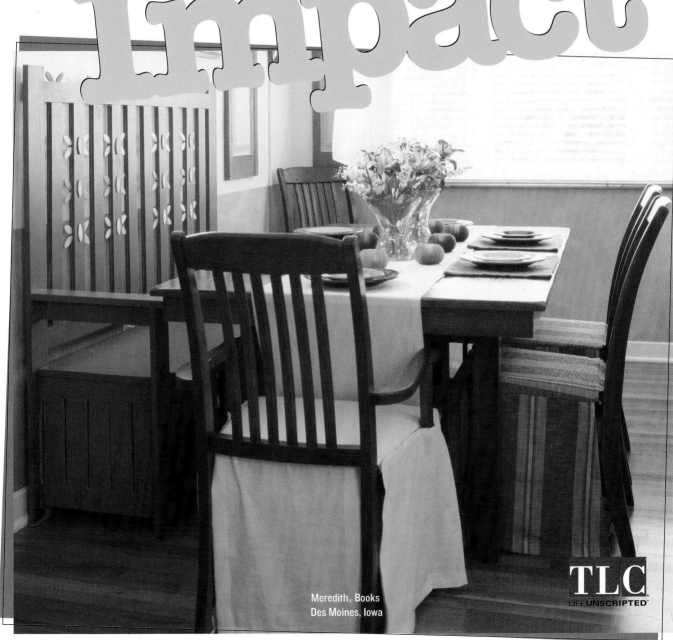

Meredith₀ Books
Des Moines, Iowa

TLC
LIFE UNSCRIPTED

Contents

Instant Impact

Editor: Amy Tincher-Durik

Senior Associate Design Director: Ken Carlson

Project Editor and Writer: Jan Soults Walker

Contributing Art Directors: Chris Conyers, Chad Johnston, Joe Wysong,
    Conyers Design, Inc.

Contributing Writers: Amber D. Barz, Jody Garlock

Contributing Project Designers: Rebecca Jerdee, Peggy Johnston,
    Gayle Schadendorf, Jim Williams

Contributing Photographers: William Hopkins, Scott Little, Paul Whicheloe
    (Anyway Productions Inc.), Jay Wilde

Illustrator: Michael Burns

Copy Chief: Terri Fredrickson

Publishing Operations Manager: Karen Schirm

Managers, Book Production: Pam Kvitne, Marjorie J. Schenkelberg,
    Rick von Holdt, Mark Weaver

Contributing Copy Editor: Jane Woychick

Contributing Proofreaders: Sue Fetters, Heidi Johnson, Brenda Scott Royce

Indexer: Kathleen Poole

Editorial Assistant: Kaye Chabot

Meredith₀ Books
Editor in Chief: Linda Raglan Cunningham

Design Director: Matt Strelecki

Managing Editor: Gregory M. Kayko

Executive Editor: Denise L. Caringer

Publisher: James D. Blume

Executive Director, Marketing: Jeffrey Myers

Executive Director, New Business Development: Todd M. Davis

Executive Director, Sales: Ken Zagor

Director, Operations: George A. Susral

Director, Production: Douglas M. Johnston

Business Director: Jim Leonard

Vice President and General Manager: Douglas J. Guendel

Meredith Publishing Group
President, Publishing Group: Stephen M. Lacy

Vice President-Publishing Director: Bob Mate

Meredith Corporation
Chairman and Chief Executive Officer: William T. Kerr

In Memoriam: E. T. Meredith III (1933—2003)

Copyright © 2004 by Meredith Corporation, Des Moines, Iowa. First Edition.
All rights reserved. Printed in the United States of America.
Library of Congress Control Number: 2004103865
ISBN: 0-696-22130-6
All of us at Meredith Books are dedicated to providing you with information and ideas
to enhance your home. We welcome your comments and suggestions. Write to us at:
Meredith Books, Home Decorating and Design Editorial Department, 1716 Locust St.,
Des Moines, IA 50309-3023.

If you would like to purchase any of our home decorating and design, cooking, crafts,
gardening, or home improvement books, check wherever quality books are sold.
Or visit us at: meredithbooks.com

Cover photograph: Paul Whicheloe (Anyway Productions Inc.)

The decorating projects and how-to instructions set forth in this book are not necessarily
endorsed or recommended by the *Trading Spaces* designers and are intended instead
to illustrate some of the basic techniques that can be used in home decorating.

Trading Spaces **Book Development Team**
Kathy Davidov, Executive Producer, TLC

Roger Marmet, Senior Vice President and General Manager, TLC

Tom Farrell, Executive Producer, Banyan Productions

Sharon M. Bennett, Senior Vice President, Strategic Partnerships & Licensing

Carol LeBlanc, Vice President, Marketing, Strategic Partnerships

Deirdre Scott, Vice President, Licensing

Elizabeth Bakacs, Creative Director, Strategic Partnerships

Erica Jacobs Green, Publishing Manager

Near the beginning of every episode of *Trading Spaces* and *Trading Spaces: Family,* Paige and Joe give four friends and two families, respectively, the keys to each other's homes. The keys unlock more than doors; they open up a fun and informative 48-hour design lesson for everyone. The neighbors learn a variety of design secrets as they transform ordinary rooms into exciting, personality-packed spaces. Throughout the episode design elements are layered in, and each instantly makes a visual impact. As the makeovers progress, it's common to hear neighbors exclaim, "Wow!" and "I would never have thought of that!" and "That is gorgeous!"

▶ Joe Farrell

With this book, you are holding the same keys as the neighbors who have appeared on-air. This is your opportunity to walk through some *Trading Spaces* rooms—at your own pace—and learn how each designer took an interior from a ho-hum "Before" to a fantastic "After." Notice how the designers use fabric, finishes, architectural details, artwork, and embellishments; their ideas will help you fill your own rooms with personality and style. Every room tour features additional design help such as suggestions on how to choose colors, create a casual dining atmosphere, and select paint sheens and fabrics.

You'll also find 15 fun, brand-new projects inspired by the show that yield eye-catching results. Every section also offers tips, tools, and techniques to help you make your room transformations in record time.

So, as Paige and Joe might say, "Here are your keys! It's time to get busy and have fun!"

Trading Spaces Treasure

Chest

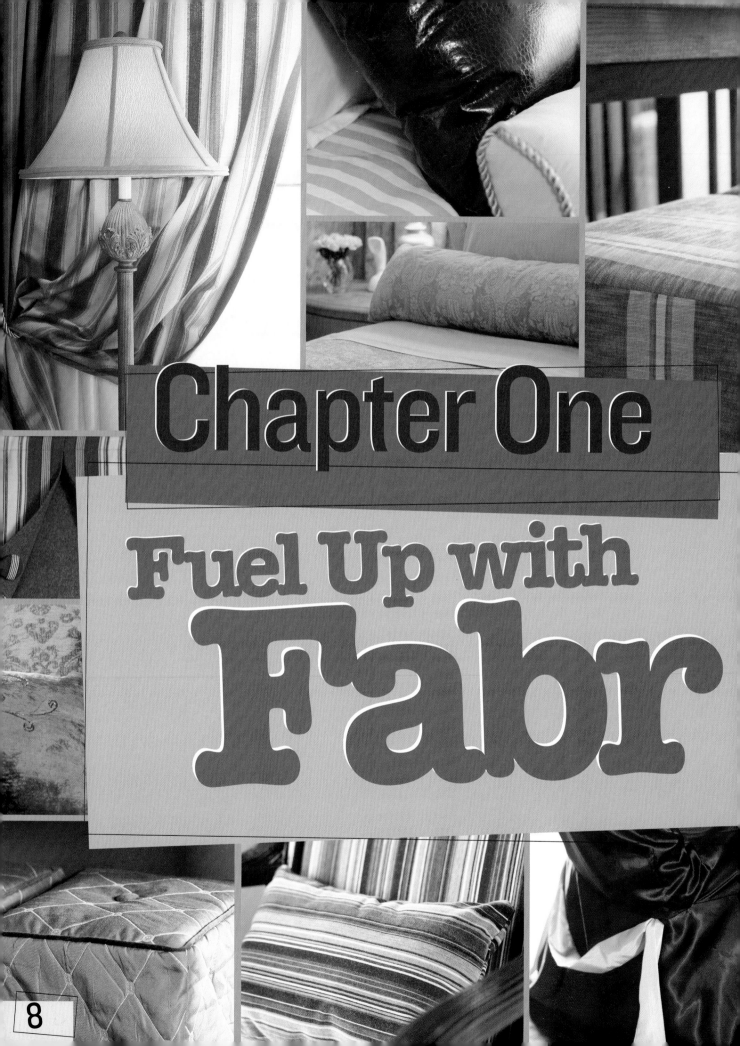

Chapter One

Fuel Up with Fabr

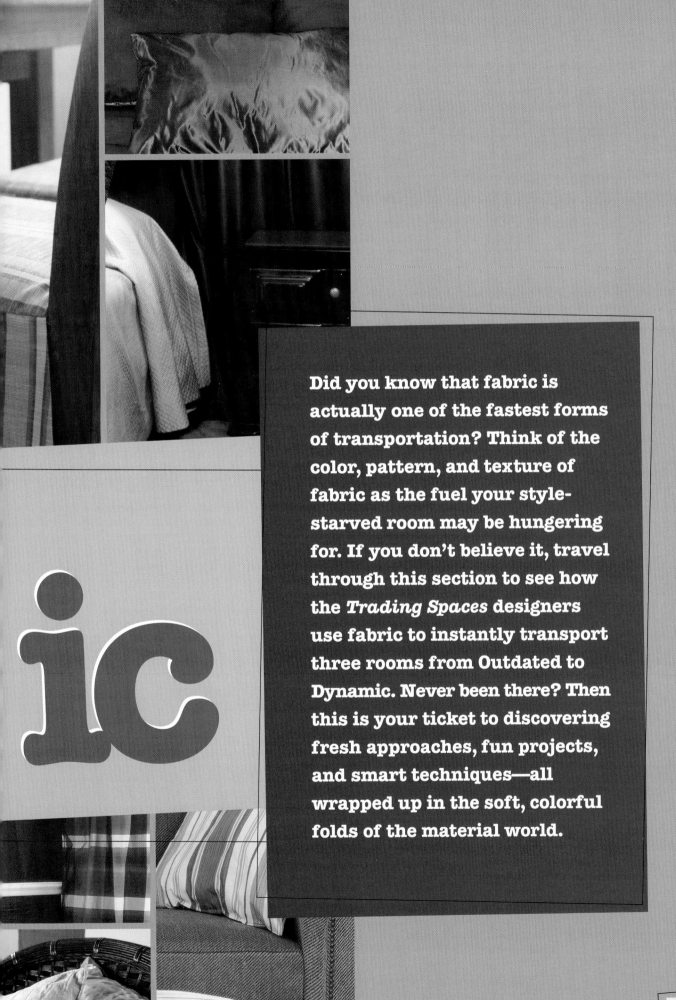

Did you know that fabric is actually one of the fastest forms of transportation? Think of the color, pattern, and texture of fabric as the fuel your style-starved room may be hungering for. If you don't believe it, travel through this section to see how the *Trading Spaces* designers use fabric to instantly transport three rooms from Outdated to Dynamic. Never been there? Then this is your ticket to discovering fresh approaches, fun projects, and smart techniques—all wrapped up in the soft, colorful folds of the material world.

Serene
Sanctuary

This master bedroom was a "stay-away" rather than a getaway until Gen stepped in to create a peaceful atmosphere. So-soft hues tastefully combine with fabric stripes and playful, unexpected doses of black vinyl to shape a tranquil yet fun retreat.

DESIGNED BY GENEVIEVE

1 LOVELY ILLUSION A band of crisp white paint creates the illusion of crown molding and requires much less time to install.

2 CLEAN LIVING Selecting a side table with uncomplicated lines enhances the stress-free style of the room.

3 CHIC STRIPES Stripes are always in style. This camel and white striped fabric—wrapped around layers of batting—turns three ordinary plywood rectangles into an appealing headboard in record time.

4 WARM-UP All-white walls left this room feeling cold and unwelcoming. Earthy taupe turns up the heat to a warm, inviting level.

5 COOL INTERLUDE A pale blue painted rectangle stakes out a spot for the new headboard and provides a cool resting place for the eyes. Molding outlines the edges.

6 GET FUNKY One extra-large pillow covered in black vinyl with a snakeskin pattern makes a sexy, shiny addition to the head of the bed.

7 REVERSE THINKING A duvet cover fashioned from solid taupe fabric on one side and camel and white stripes on the other ties the bed to the serene color scheme.

8 EVEN GLOW Matching lamps offer bedside symmetry and balanced lighting.

before

When it comes to fabric, some of the most striking companions aren't always the obvious choices. Gen successfully teams the unexpected in this master bedroom using camel and white stripes, solid taupe cotton, and playful black vinyl to give an ordinary mattress and box springs star status.

Before tackling the bed, Gen begins with a few giggles when she reveals that the lovely warm taupe paint color she has chosen for the walls is called "Squirrel." Despite the somewhat oddball label, the hue instantly makes this space a cozy retreat from the outside world. Gen also uses paint to create several clever architectural illusions, such as bands of white at the top and bottom of each wall that mimic crown

▲ A mirror in a golden frame replaces a shattered dresser mirror. The black vinyl cushions at the foot of the bed top a pair of custom-made cubes.

◀ Large carpet squares featuring a geometric pattern are positioned so that the pattern is random, creating an exciting work of art underfoot. Rubber backing eliminates the need to lay padding first, and adhesive dots speed installation. Tension keeps the squares snug. To complement the contemporary flooring, the window treatment is casual, loosely knotted for a fast yet stylish finish.

◀ A low custom-built cabinet provides a place for the homeowners' books and other belongings. Prefabricated storage cubes can be stacked in minutes to achieve a similar setup. For artwork, wedding photos are mounted on blue rectangles painted on the walls. The backs of the matted frames were removed so that when the frames were mounted on the wall, the blue background would show through.

◄An overstuffed black vinyl pillow provides an unexpected element on the bed. Leather and felt are also good choices for fast fabric projects such as accent pillows. When these materials are cut, the raw edges don't fray, so no hemming is necessary.

and base moldings. A rectangle of pale blue outlines a new location for the bed, and authentic moldings define the blue expanse.

Within the field of blue, a new headboard provides a soft backrest. It's made from three plywood rectangles wrapped in batting and covered with the striped fabric. Topping the bed is a reversible duvet cover fashioned from two fabrics: dark taupe on one side and a camel and white stripe on the other side. Pillows in crisp white and taupe keep company with one overstuffed pillow covered in black vinyl that features a fun snakeskin pattern.

One of the homeowners wished for a place to store books, and Gen fulfills the request with a long, low bookcase, custom-made by Amy Wynn. Black vinyl cushions top custom-built cubes at the foot of the bed, offering a comfy place to sit.

Instead of laying ordinary new carpet to replace the old, Gen finds 18×18-inch carpet squares with a geometric pattern. She decides to place the squares randomly, so the new pattern that results is as fresh as an abstract work of art.

The couple's wedding photos, a fitting romantic touch, complete the transformation with quiet elegance.

◄Hook-and-loop tape secures these headboard rectangles to the wall and will allow easy removal when a change of fabric is desired. Both installation and removal take only a few minutes, allowing maximum versatility and frequent style updates.

Nightstand Nuances

Bedside storage space is a smart convenience. Choose yours intelligently, using these tips:

▶ Nightstands are necessary with many bed styles and are most convenient when they stand a few inches taller than the height of the mattress—about 27 to 33 inches high. Evaluate how you'll use the nightstand and what you will store. Tissues, eyeglasses, and books are easier to reach when stored on shelves rather than in drawers.

▶ If you use medications or items that you would like to keep out of sight, choose a nightstand with at least one drawer. Consider whether the top is large enough to hold an alarm clock, a decorative item, and perhaps a telephone. If the room has no fixed lighting beside the bed, you will also need space for a small table lamp. Choose nightstands that complement the bed size and style; an exact match isn't necessary. Small chests work well beside twin beds. King-size beds require something heftier.

▶ For guest room nightstands, drawers and shelves are optional; short-term visitors aren't likely to store items in them. Use a vintage table or a small chest perhaps borrowed from another room.

▲Even if you're a novice sewer, you can stitch this easy headboard slipcover in an afternoon. To simplify the project even more, eliminate the decorative piping.

Headboard Cover-Up

Put a flea market headboard under wraps with fabric chosen to beautify your boudoir.

▶ **MATERIALS**
Fabrics (for slipcover front, lining, and piping)
Cording, #0, ⁵⁄₃₂-inch
Matching thread

▶ **TOOLS**
Fabric tape measure
Scissors
Iron and ironing board
Sewing machine
Straight pins
Zipper foot for sewing machine

Measure the width of the headboard. To determine the slipcover length, use a fabric tape measure; start at the back lower edge where the headboard meets the mattress. Draw the tape up and over the top of the headboard and measure down to the top of the mattress. Add 1 inch to the width and 2 inches to the length measurement for the seam allowance.

Cut two fabric pieces to size (one piece in decorator fabric and one lining piece).

If desired, make piping (A), following the instructions *below*, in a length that equals the perimeter of the cut decorator fabric.

Cut eight 3×15-inch strips for the fabric ties. Press the long edges under to make a 1-inch-wide tie. Topstitch the edges.

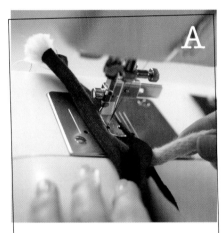

The Perfect Piping

Here's how to make your own piping: Cover soft cord with bias-cut fabric strips as follows: Cut a square yard of fabric. Fold diagonally, wrong side out. Now you have a triangle. Measure 1 ¼ inches from the fold, creating a parallel line. Mark additional parallel lines 2 ½ inches apart. Mark and cut these strips until they are less than a foot long. Discard the remnants. Align the short diagonal ends of the strips and sew right sides together to form a long straight strip, or casing. With the casing wrong side up, lay the cord along the center. Fold the casing over the cord; stitch close to the cord using a zipper foot (A). After layering the slipcover front and back, as instructed, pin the piping around the edges of the fabric layers, aligning raw edges and overlapping the ends; stitch.

Lay the slipcover front flat, right side up, and fold in half widthwise to find the center. Use pins to mark the center on each edge. Unfold the fabric. To determine where to position the ties along the edges, measure 10 and 20 inches above and below the center and mark these points with pins: four pins on the top portion and four on the bottom portion.

Place the backing fabric on top of the slipcover front, right sides together; position the piping and ties between the layers and pin them in place.

Stitch a ½-inch seam allowance on the two long sides using a zipper foot (B), removing the pins as you stitch. Stitch one end of the slipcover with a 1-inch seam allowance. Turn the slipcover right side out. Press the perimeter of the slipcover and turn under 1 inch on the open edge. Topstitch to close.

Place the slipcover over the headboard and tie in place (C).

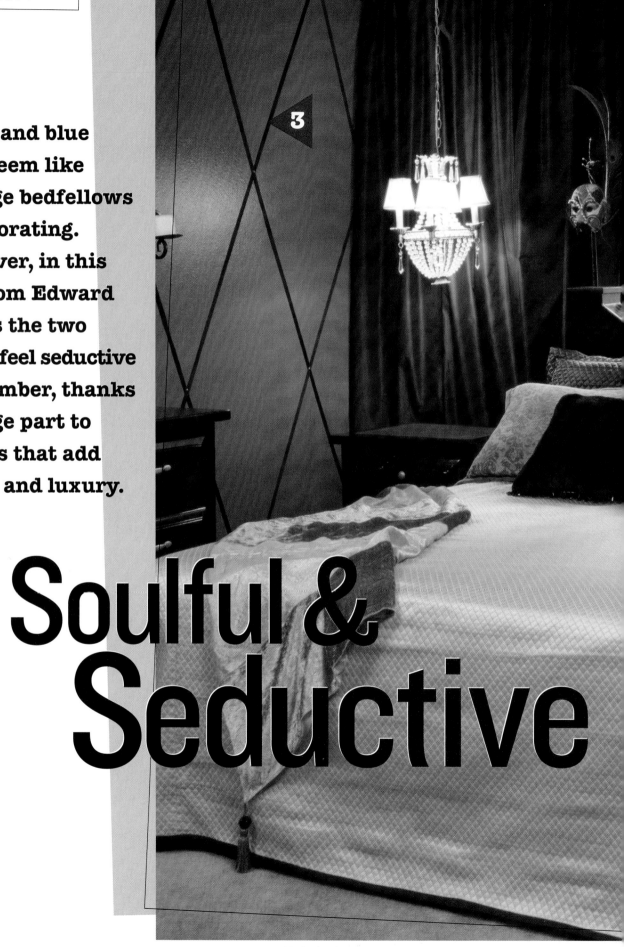

Black and blue may seem like strange bedfellows in decorating. However, in this bedroom Edward makes the two colors feel seductive not somber, thanks in large part to fabrics that add luster and luxury.

Soulful & Seductive

3

1 GOLDEN TOUCH Fabric can be a gold mine for your decorating makeovers. This shimmering golden bedspread keeps the room from becoming dark and dungeonlike.

2 DO THE TWIST With a few tweaks, an ordinary item can become exceptional. These two Roman shades are pulled up in the centers to form curves that follow the contours of the headboard. The tassels echo the golden tone of the bedspread.

3 CROSSING OVER For pattern without much commitment or effort, adorn a wall with ribbon. Hung on the diagonal, these ribbons crisscross to form a stylish harlequin pattern (much faster than a paint job). The ribbons tack into place at the top and bottom and at intersections to keep the design secure.

4 CURTAIN CALL Deep blue fabric panels soften the wall behind the bed, adding drama and intrigue. Hung right below the crown molding, the panels also give the room a sense of grandeur.

5 LUXE LOOKS Fabrics have distinct personalities and can set the tone for an entire room. The mix of fabrics used for these pillows is all about refinement and luxury.

6 FANCY THAT Chandeliers replace bedside lamps. The dark fabric panels on the wall accentuate their glittering details.

DESIGNED BY **EDWARD**

before

▶ New Orleans: Melrose Drive

This bedroom needs a wake-up call. It doesn't have much color, and the walls are almost entirely bare. Further, the furnishings are nondescript, and the arrangement limits their impact. Edward plans to bring color into the room through paint and fabrics. The furniture will be refreshed with paint and repositioned so the bed becomes the focal point of the room. And that microwave cart holding the TV? "It is gone!" Edward says.

▶Whether your art comes in the form of a mask on a dowel or a Picasso on the wall, it's worthy of a spotlight. Edward had this pillar outfitted with an uplight to cast dramatic shadows on the custom sculpture. To accent an object with lighting, choose a bulb that's about three times brighter than the general lighting in the room.

The owners of this bedroom agree that the space needs a big change. Exactly how big the change should be is up for debate. Edward opts for a bold transformation, using colors associated with a powerful punch. He douses the room with black and blue, and seemingly swept up with the New Orleans voodoo vibe, he accessorizes the space with a devilish painting and Mardi Gras masks.

In the wrong hands, the deep tones could have made the room mournful. With Edward's expert guidance, however, the room becomes soulful and seductive. Elegant fabrics steer the space toward a romantic getaway.

Yards and yards of sumptuous fabrics shimmer and shine against the blue walls and the black moldings and furnishings. A golden bedspread sparkles in the darkness, drawing the eye to the bed, which is repositioned against a window to become the focal point. Deep blue iridescent panels flow from ceiling height, creating a majestic backdrop for the bed by day and an intimate cocoon by night. The room has

◀Painted black, this newly installed crown molding finishes the room in dramatic fashion, visually connecting with the ribbons on the wall and the painted furnishings. To keep black from dragging down a room, use a high-gloss paint that reflects light.

▶The beauty of these fabrics is in their restraint. Tone-on-tone motifs, including the beadwork on the blue pillow, introduce pattern quietly and subtly. Lush textures create visual interest.

►Edward painted this devilish image on black artist's canvas. "It's a guardian to ward off evil spirits," he explains.

▼Black Roman shades with tone-on-tone stripes peacefully coexist with the deep blue panels. The unlikely color combination gives the room a sense of intrigue.

◄ It wouldn't be New Orleans without beads. This elegant beaded chandelier, though, is a striking contrast to the beads tossed around during Mardi Gras. Beads of that variety adorn the mask.

a surprisingly gentle nature, exhibited by plush fabrics with opulent textures and subtle tone-on-tone designs that exude richness and comfort.

Edward unwinds the boldest pattern from a spool rather than a bolt: Narrow ribbon tacked to the wall crisscrosses to form a large harlequin pattern. The dark ribbon pops against the blue wall. When the owners are ready for a change, "it can come right off," Edward says.

Similarly, they can swap out the masks and artwork for a completely different look. For now, this fabulous room is filled with sumptuous New Orleans-style flavor.

Say It with Fabric

There's more to fabrics than color and pattern. Like people, fabrics have personality. They can radiate warmth, exude confidence, or convey an easygoing attitude. Consider the qualities of these popular fabrics:

▶ **Brocade** has a raised pattern resembling embroidery. It's often used in formal upholstery.

▶ **Chenille** has thick needle-punched designs. Its nubby texture is suitable for casual upholstery.

▶ **Chintz** is a plain-weave glazed or unglazed cotton. It sets a traditional mood and often has a floral motif.

▶ **Damask** comes in various fibers and weights and features a satin-and-matte textural contrast. Use it for formal draperies and upholstery, or let it go casual as a loose-fitting slipcover.

▶ **Matelassé** has an elegant embossed look. It's commonly used for bedcovers.

▶ **Moiré** is known for its shimmering finish resembling watermarks or wood grain. It lends a traditional look to a room.

▶ **Taffeta** is a crisp plain-weave fabric. It works well for formal window treatments because it retains its shape with little support.

▶ **Tapestry** has thick weaves and pictorial designs. It is best suited for uncomplicated upholstery or flat window panels.

▶ **Toile de Jouy** is a tightly woven fabric with a pictorial print, usually on a white or cream background. It can look formal or casual, depending on the fabrics and furnishings that surround it.

▲Cutout designs along the edges of hemstitch table runners make perfect eyelets for leather strapping. This bolster features runners in three tasty colors: kiwi, chocolate, and boysenberry.

24

Make a Bolster

You need only minimal sewing skills to assemble this attractive triangular bolster cleverly fashioned from four hemstitch table runners.

Choose table runners that feature a hemstitch design along the edges. The hemstitch slots are ideal eyelets for lacing the pieces together with leather strapping.

Have a triangular pillow form cut to fit at an upholstery shop. To determine the size of the form needed, measure the width of the area between the decorative hemstitch slots (A). Cover the foam pillow form with batting.

To cover the ends, create a triangular paper pattern to match the bolster end. Divide this pattern into three equal triangles. Lay the paper triangles on top of the fourth table runner so that the long edge of each triangle aligns with the hemstitching on the runner. Cut out six fabric triangles (three for each end of the bolster), cutting ½ inch above each short side of the triangular pattern pieces (for

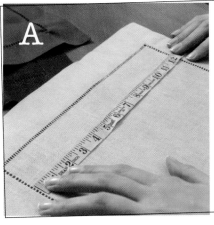

A

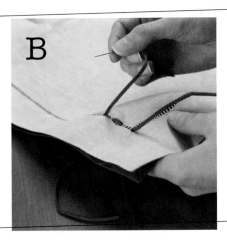

B

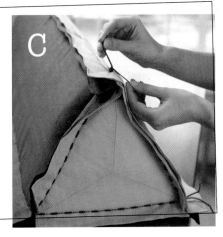

C

Position two runners over two sides of the foam triangle, aligning the hemstitching. Lace the runners together using a long, dull needle to thread leather strapping through the hemstitching (B). Thread the strapping through every third or fourth slot. Leave 3 or 4 inches of leather strap hanging at each end. Lace the third runner to the first two runners, using the same method.

seam allowance). Sew three triangular pieces together (hand-stitch or use a sewing machine) to form each bolster end piece; hand-stitch near the hemstitch ends so that the raw edges don't show. Lace each end to the bolster by threading leather strapping through the hemstitch slots. Tie off the leather strapping at the corners (C).

The Runners-Up
Select only one color for the entire pillow or mix it up as shown here. These runners measure I5 inches wide and 54 inches long; other widths and lengths are available. Look for table runners in specialty linen stores or online. Use the key search phrase "table runners" to find online retailers. Then search the site for hemstitch runners. To personalize your pillow, search for an online retailer that offers free monogramming.

Luxury Liner

Edward relies on nautical flags—and the colors and motifs gleaned from them—to send a clear signal on this yacht: Classic style is here to stay.

DESIGNED BY EDWARD

1 SECRET CODE Whenever you have a chance to personalize your decorating, do it. Though used for decorative purposes indoors, these nautical signal flags still send out a message in a flash. Each flag represents a letter of the alphabet. When decoded, the flags spell out the name of the motor yacht. This checked flag represents the letter "N"; the yacht is named My Lady Enna.

2 EASY LIVING Take a cue from this sofa: Make cushions from easy-care fabrics. These cushions wear vinyl covers that have a waterproof backing to withstand spills or wet swimsuits. Similar wipe-to-clean fabrics also work well in landlocked playrooms.

3 SOMETHING'S FISHY You have to walk a fine line to find things that appeal to both kids and adults. This dolphin coffee table adds splash in the playroom—it's fun for all ages.

4 SET SAIL Repurposing is so much better when it has meaning. This coffee table is made of wooden pieces from an old boat.

5 CLASS ACT Valances are the little curtains that could. Though requiring only a bit of fabric, they can dramatically alter the look of a room. These striped valances draw the eye to the best feature: the windows and the view they frame.

6 OUTDOOR/INDOOR Chairs made for outdoors can look right at home when brought inside, especially in a casual setting. New creamy white cushions and red, white, and blue pillows brighten this brown patio chair and its mate.

27

► Edward built this banquette from teakwood salvaged from an old boat. It maximizes seating in the salon and offers bonus storage space underneath. The deep tones of red and blue used in all the rooms create a sophisticated look that pure primary colors would not achieve. New ceiling lights update the setting.

When a house comes in the form of a big boat, the decorating challenges are many. The durability of all materials and the weight of every object must be considered, and of course, space is limited. "It's a decent-size room because it's a 56-foot boat, but it's still not a house," one of the owners says of the primary living spaces on this motor yacht.

Indeed, Edward has his work cut out for him when he captains the makeover of the yacht salon, dinette, and enclosed deck that's used as a playroom. Harsh sunlight, moisture, and cramped quarters are his main adversaries. The yacht's owners have requested that the mahogany walls and woodwork remain untouched.

Painting walls is typically a designer's first order of business. With the walls off-limits, Edward sets his classic design afloat with fabrics. Nylon nautical flags—primarily in red, white, and blue, with touches of yellow and black—inspire the fabric colors and

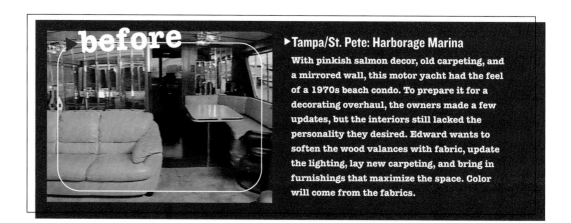

before

► **Tampa/St. Pete: Harborage Marina**
With pinkish salmon decor, old carpeting, and a mirrored wall, this motor yacht had the feel of a 1970s beach condo. To prepare it for a decorating overhaul, the owners made a few updates, but the interiors still lacked the personality they desired. Edward wants to soften the wood valances with fabric, update the lighting, lay new carpeting, and bring in furnishings that maximize the space. Color will come from the fabrics.

▲Painted half red and half blue, this dining table mimics a nautical flag signifying the letter E. The blue vinyl seat cushions make it easy to wipe up spills or accommodate kids in wet swimsuits; vinyl is a stylishly seaworthy option and is available in many colors at fabrics stores. The striped fabric used for the valance repeats on the back cushions.

designs. A striped fabric and complementary solid color bring natty nautical style into the salon and dinette. Designed for outdoor use, the fabrics resist fading, moisture, and mildew. Vinyl fabrics with a waterproof backing turn seat cushions into easy-care surfaces. Pillows with creamy white backgrounds and bold geometric designs—actually flag symbols—are tossed about the yacht, providing instant color and a casual contrast to the rich mahogany wood.

The nautical flags become a fun focal point in the playroom, which flows from the salon. The flags are international symbols that ships use to communicate with one another; their clean-lined designs represent a letter or word. Edward hangs twelve flags near the playroom ceiling to spell out the name of the yacht: "My Lady Enna MY" (motor yacht).

Though the owners don't immediately connect the flags to a special message, they're buoyed by Edward's design, which evokes the classic look of a 1920s luxury liner. "We couldn't have asked for a better design," one owner says. "Edward really did a great job of researching a nautical lifestyle."

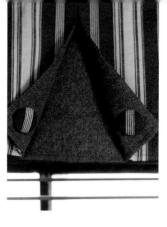

▲With kicky box pleats, this valance has tailored good looks. The pleats were easily created by stitching rectangles of blue fabric between striped pieces of fabric. The blue fabric insets are then folded in to form the look of box pleats. Flaps are then pulled back at the seam to reveal the complementary blue fabric. Buttons covered in the striped fabric and attached to the pulled-back portion are strictly decorative. The fabric valance covers a mahogany predecessor, visually softening the setting. Hook-and-loop tape made installation quick and easy and eliminated worries about damaging the wood valance.

▶Projects made from MDF (medium-density fiberboard) would have been too heavy for the boat, so Edward decided to salvage woods that had already been deemed boatworthy. Fortunately, the areas by marinas are usually filled with goodies that can be great finds for nautical-style rooms. Edward turned swim platforms and a mast from an old sailboat into this coffee table. The weathered wood is a striking contrast to the rich mahogany walls and trim.

▼A faux finish gives this wall behind the banquette depth. It's a visually pleasing departure from the mirrors that once covered this surface.

◄Shipshape pillows bring the nautical-flag theme into the salon and visually soften the banquette cushion, which can be wiped clean with a damp rag.

Fabric Roles

Before spending money on a fabric you think you can't live without, consider where you plan to use it and the role you want it to play. A lustrous moiré, for example, is unmistakably formal and would look awkward in a casual setting. Similarly, a heavy canvas would work great for a roll-up shade; however, it lacks the drape required for pleated curtain panels. To avoid costly mistakes, ask yourself a few questions before splurging:

▶ **What's your climate?** This is especially important to consider if you're choosing drapery fabrics and you live in an unusually sunny or a cold climate; natural fibers trap heat, and light-color, tightly woven opaque fabrics reflect sunlight. If humidity is a factor, look for fibers with less absorbency.

▶ **What's your goal?** If you want long-lasting, easy-care, soil- and stain-resistant upholstery, look for cleanable fabrics that have protective finishes. Or apply a spray-on finish yourself. Easier yet, check out the wide selection of weather-resistant fabrics designed for outdoor use—they're suitable for many indoor applications too.

▶ **What's the end use?** Put the right fabrics to work in the right places by keeping these general guidelines in mind: Fabrics that work well for upholstery include chintz and cotton for light upholstery; chenille and wool for medium-weight upholstery; and brocade and damask for heavier upholstery. Good drapery fabrics include lightly glazed chintz, lightweight to medium-weight cotton, and silk.

◀ Wrapped in windows, this playroom has a magnificent view. Thanks to Edward, the room itself is pleasant to view. It functions well as a playroom yet is stylish enough for adults to enjoy. The sofa is covered in kid-friendly fabric that wipes clean. The blue seat cushion and the yellow back cushion are a playful combination.

▶ **MATERIALS**

Striped fabric (enough yardage to cover two-thirds of the wall height as well as the width of the wall)

Ready-made wall upholstery tape or a roll of 2-inch-wide kraft-paper painter's tape (to make your own upholstery tape)

Moldings (for top and corners of wainscoting)

Paint (for moldings)

Finishing nails

▶ **TOOLS**

Pencil

Carpenter's level

Tape measure

Fabric marking pen

T square

Scissors

Iron and ironing board

Staple gun and staples

Hammer

▲Vertically striped fabric and painted moldings lend graphic appeal to this ordinary wall. Adding a second narrow board across the top piece of molding gives this accent wall a ledge for displaying woven trays.

Cover a Wall with Fabric

Bring pattern and a soft accent to a plain wall with this upholstered wainscoting. Moldings hide raw fabric edges at top and bottom for a quick finish.

Remove any existing base molding from the wall. Using a pencil and a carpenter's level, mark a horizontal guideline across the wall approximately two-thirds of the way above the floor. Also use these tools to mark a plumb line in each corner of the wall; these will serve as vertical guides for keeping the stripes straight.

Place the fabric on a work surface. Measure the desired lengths and use a fabric marking pen and a T square to establish cutting lines that are square with the long edges of the fabric. Cut the panels to length; press.

Have a helper assist you in hanging the fabric. For the first panel, begin at the left side of the accent wall. Have the helper hold the panel against the adjacent wall, with the right side of the fabric facing that wall. Slide the panel toward the accent wall and fold the first stripe under; align the long edge of the folded stripe with the plumb line and use the horizontal guideline to position the top corner of the fabric. Line the back of the folded stripe with upholstery tape (to make your own upholstery tape, see instructions on this page). Staple through the tape and the folded-under stripe (A), evenly spacing staples every 2 or 3 inches from top to bottom.

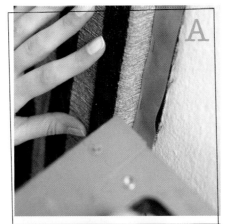

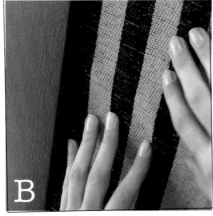

After stapling, fold the fabric panel over the stapled edge so that the right side of the fabric is facing out (B). Hold the panel flat against the wall to see where the right edge ends; before stapling further, use a carpenter's level and a pencil to mark a plumb line on the wall as a visual gauge to keep the stripes straight.

With stripes aligned, staple across the panel top, spacing staples every 2 or 3 inches. Be careful not to stretch the fabric.

For the second panel, repeat the procedure used for the first panel; lay the first stripe on top of the last stripe of the previous panel so that the right sides of the fabric panels are facing.

Repeat the procedure with each fabric panel to cover the accent wall. Finish the right edge of the last panel by folding the fabric under to align with the last plumb line. Strengthen the right edge with a lining of upholstery tape and staple the edge in place.

Paint all moldings to match; let dry. Reattach the base molding (or purchase base molding if none was present) with finishing nails and a hammer. The molding will hide the bottom raw edges of the fabric. Add top molding to cover the top raw edges, then install a narrow plate ledge, if desired. Use corner molding to conceal the staples along the right edge of the accent wall.

Upholstery Tape Substitute

Make your own upholstery tape using strips of kraft-paper painter's tape. Cut the strips to match the length of the fabric panels. Fold the tape in half lengthwise (sticky side in); press the fold with your fingertips to create a firm edge. Use the folded piece of tape as a sturdy backing for the long edges of the fabric panels being stapled to the wall.

More Fun with Fabric

Basic Stitches

Find a machine that makes these six stitches and you're ready to undertake an assortment of fabric projects:

Buttonholes. Create closures for medium-weight to heavyweight fabrics using keyhole or square-end styles.

Blind stitch. Use this stitch to create invisible hems in woven fabrics and medium-weight to heavyweight stretch fabrics.

Satin stitch. Employ this wide stitch to secure appliqués to fabric or use it as decorative trim.

Zigzag stitch. Switch to this stitch when you're ready to attach trims or finish seams.

Basting stitch. This long, straight stitch is ideal for gathering fabric or for temporary closures.

Straight stitch. You may find yourself using this basic stitch most often. Use it to join all weights of woven fabrics.

Use this primer to learn what to look for in a sewing machine. Study a few basic machine stitches that come in handy for all kinds of projects on *Trading Spaces*. Peruse some common fabric terms and have fun learning to make pillows. Or, if you don't want to sew, take a look at fusible webbing and other no-sew project materials.

Tips for Success

MATCHING REPEATS
Did you know that the selvage edge on patterned fabric reveals the length of the motif repeat? Use the distance between these marks to determine how much extra fabric to buy. The marks will also help you align the pattern when you're joining two lengths of the same patterned fabric side by side.

Sewing Machine Savvy

Keep these 10 tips in mind when you shop for a sewing machine:

1) Have an idea of the types of projects you want to sew, such as window treatments and pillows. If the projects you plan to sew are fairly simple, then basic features are all you'll need.

2) Prices range from about $200 to thousands of dollars. Purchase the best machine you can afford, tempering your choice with a fair assessment of how often you'll use it.

3) Research various brands and try them at the store before you buy.

4) Inspect stitch quality on a variety of fabric types.

5) Experiment with different types of stitches, such as zigzag, buttonholes, and decorative stitches.

6) Make your purchase from a reputable dealer and ask if classes are available.

7) To ensure that your machine will be repaired correctly, seek a dealer that offers in-house service.

8) Look for special machine features recommended by experienced sewers: a thread cutter, a needle threader, auto-tension, and an auto-buttonholer. All the other features are a bonus or unnecessary, depending on the type of sewing you plan to do.

9) Ask the salesperson lots of questions and take notes on the features you like on the different machines.

10) Ask for the names of customers who can serve as references. Contact them to find out their opinions on the performance of a specific machine.

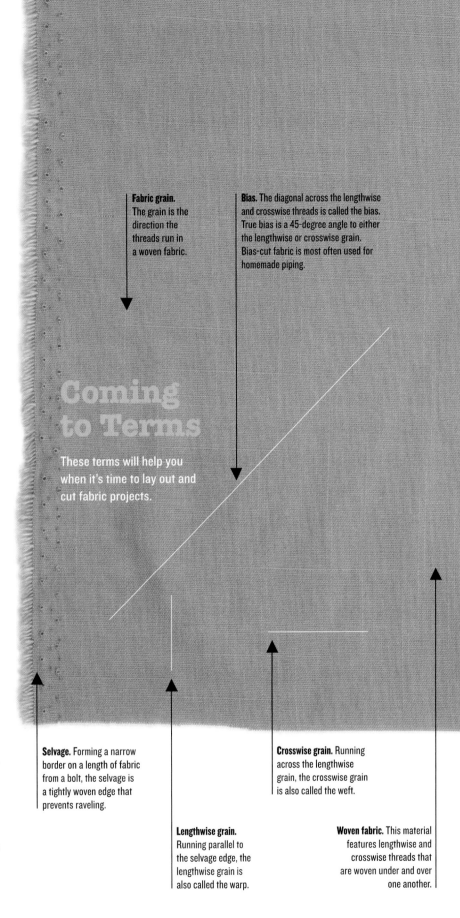

Fabric grain. The grain is the direction the threads run in a woven fabric.

Bias. The diagonal across the lengthwise and crosswise threads is called the bias. True bias is a 45-degree angle to either the lengthwise or crosswise grain. Bias-cut fabric is most often used for homemade piping.

Coming to Terms

These terms will help you when it's time to lay out and cut fabric projects.

Selvage. Forming a narrow border on a length of fabric from a bolt, the selvage is a tightly woven edge that prevents raveling.

Lengthwise grain. Running parallel to the selvage edge, the lengthwise grain is also called the warp.

Crosswise grain. Running across the lengthwise grain, the crosswise grain is also called the weft.

Woven fabric. This material features lengthwise and crosswise threads that are woven under and over one another.

35

Sew-Simple Pillows

Two fabric sides, matching thread, a pillow form, and some piping if desired—these are the basic ingredients for whipping up a decorative pillow at home. Here are some options:

Closed Cover

This cover is stitched closed around the pillow form and remains in place until you rip the seams and re-cover the form with another fabric.

1) Measure the pillow form and add 1 inch when you cut the fabric. For example, if you're using an 18-inch-square pillow form, cut a front and a back piece 19 inches square.

2) If your pillow won't have piping, skip to step 3. Cut enough 1½-inch-wide bias strips to make piping for your pillow. Follow the directions on page 17 to make the piping. Starting with one fabric piece, right side up, align the raw edge of the piping with the raw edges on the fabric. Begin laying the piping in the center along one edge and pin the piping in place all the way around the fabric piece. Where the ends of the piping meet, pull back an inch or so of the fabric around the piping cord and cut the ends of the cord to abut. Refold one end of the fabric cover over the cord. On the remaining end, turn under the raw edge of the cover and refold the fabric around the cord. Use a zipper foot on the sewing machine to baste the piping to the fabric panel.

3) Place the pillow front and back right sides together; pin. Trim the corners of the fabric pieces on the diagonal (A). Stitch the front and back together using a straight stitch and a ½-inch seam allowance. (If your pillow has piping, use a zipper foot and stitch along the basting line.) Leave one side of the pillow open for turning. Press seams.

4) Turn the pillow cover right side out and push the corners out. Press corners. Slip the pillow form into the cover and whipstitch the opening closed by hand (B).

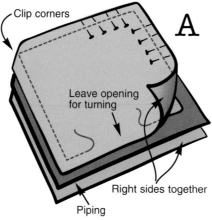

Clip corners

Leave opening for turning

A

Right sides together

Piping

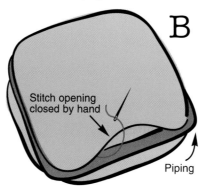

B

Stitch opening closed by hand

Piping

Sham-Style Cover

This pillow cover—also called a French flap—features a slot on the back that lets you remove the pillow form and wash the cover. The style makes it easy to change the look of a room to suit the seasons or your mood.

1) Starting with an 18-inch-square pillow form, cut one front piece of fabric 19 inches square.

2) Cut two back pieces of fabric, each measuring 19×14 inches. On one long edge of one of the back pieces, fold the fabric under ½ inch and press. Then fold the fabric under 1 inch, press, and straight-stitch to hem. Repeat with the second back fabric piece. These two hemmed edges will later become the slot for inserting the pillow.

3) Lay the front piece of fabric on a work surface right side up. Lay the two back pieces on top of the front piece with the right sides facing down, aligning the raw edges of the front and back pieces. Position the back pieces in the center so that the hemmed edges are overlapping to form the slot for the pillow form (C opposite). (The hemmed edges will overlap about 2½ inches.)

4) Check that all edges are even; pin in place. Stitch around the pillow, using a ½-inch seam allowance. Trim corners on the diagonal (D opposite).

5) Turn the pillow cover right side out and press. Insert the pillow form and fluff (E opposite).

OPTIONAL: To add piping to this pillow, pin the piping to the front piece in step 3. Then continue with the rest of the directions.

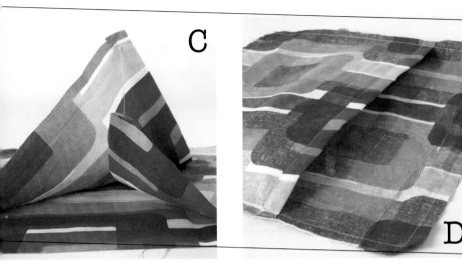

C

D

E

The No-Sew Option

If you prefer not to sew, put away the thread and needle and use iron-on fusible webbing or fusible tape instead to secure hems and seams:

Fusible tape comes in various widths that suit lots of different projects. For example, relatively narrow tape lets you bond wide ribbon to bed linens. Sheets of fusible webbing (shown at the back of the photograph) allow you to secure appliqués to pillow fronts.

Besides fusible webbing or tape, keep an iron, scissors, and a cloth measuring tape on hand for your no-sew projects.

Wash and dry the fabric first, then cut the tape or webbing to size and follow the directions on the package to join the fabric pieces. In most cases, lay the iron-on adhesive strip or sheet between the fabric layers and press the layers with an iron turned to a low-heat setting; hold the iron in place for the recommended amount of time.

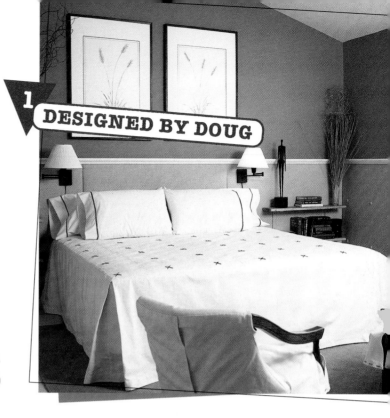

1 DESIGNED BY DOUG

Fabric
Favorites

Some designs are worth seeing again and again. These popular *Trading Spaces* rooms highlight clever fabric strategies that can help you create styles ranging from playful to elegant.

2 DESIGNED BY HILDI

3 DESIGNED BY VERN

4 DESIGNED BY FRANK

1 SOFTEN SURROUNDINGS If you love a bedroom that makes you feel as cozy as a warm blanket, then you'll appreciate the glow Doug brings to this bedroom from Indiana: Fieldhurst Lane. Playing off deep orange walls, Doug mixes in soft contrasting hues and textural elements by creating an upholstered wainscoting of gray heavy-weave cotton fabric. Fabric-covered buttons lend appealing detail to the wall and make the treatment appear even more plush. White linens on the bed—dressed up with ribbon accents— and white canvas slipcovers on a pair of chairs add a fresh, airy touch that balances the high-temperature wall color.

2 COLOR SOME FUN Hildi employs yards of playful pink python-print vinyl to cover this 11-foot-long custom-made sofa in Philadelphia: Cresheim Road. Sparkling fabric pillows and velvety

floor-to-ceiling draperies (behind the sofa) deliver doses of luxury and glamour to this combination sitting room/office.

3 GO FOR GLAMOUR In San Clemente: Camino Mojado, Vern transforms a plain loft into a glamorous media room. Diamond-shape plywood pieces, elegantly upholstered in taupe and black fabrics, give the space 1930s Hollywood style. The batting-and-fabric-covered plywood panels are practical for this type of room because they absorb sound and are comfortable to lean against. Rather than permanently affixing them to the wall, Vern uses hook-and-loop tape. If the fabric on one piece becomes stained or damaged, the panel can be removed and the fabric replaced.

4 SHAPE YOUR STYLE Plywood becomes shapely works of art when you take a cue from

Frank in Miramar: Avenue 164. The red walls of this bedroom are bold and welcoming. However, Frank's unorthodox headboard is what gives the space real pizzazz. It's made from various plywood shapes wrapped in batting and different solid-color fabrics. Hook-and-loop tape secures the shapes to the wall, allowing easy removal in the future. The result is a funky, retro atmosphere.

5 ADD ADVENTURE If you have your eye on a pricey fabric, borrow Kia's adventurous design tricks from Indianapolis: Halleck Way. She found incredible fabric with an Egyptian motif for $69 a yard. Rather than let it go, Kia bought what she could afford and employs the piece as a dramatic backdrop for the bed. Other fabrics in the room— a silky bedspread, velvet on the headboard, and sheer curtain panels—play off the jewel tones established by her smart splurge.

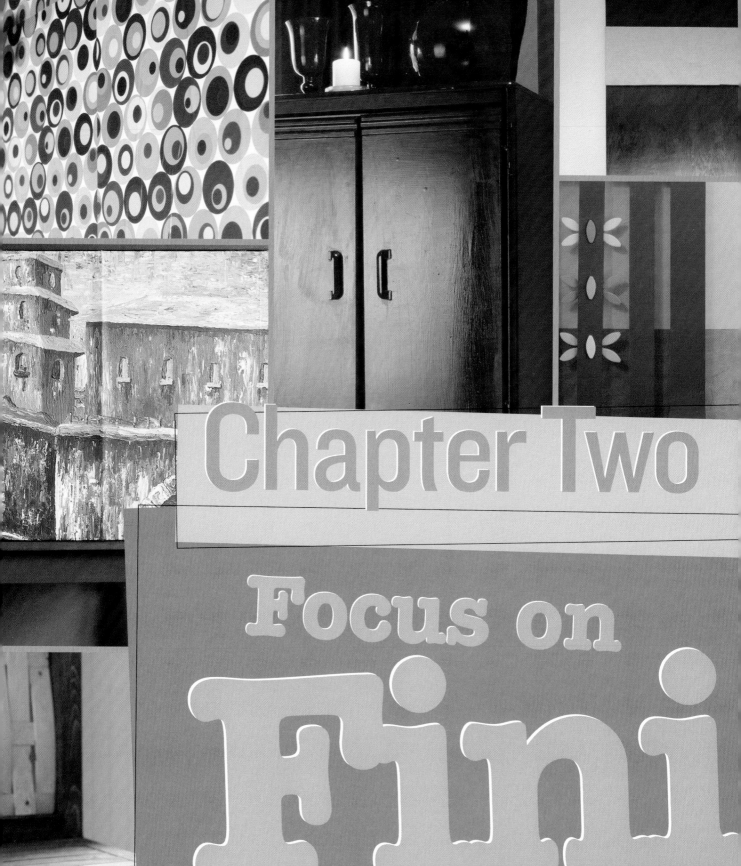

Chapter Two

Focus on
Fini

Wondering whether the surfaces in your rooms are subtle or just plain sleepy? If you have to ask, it's time to liven up the party. No surface need suffer the indignity of being ignored. Take your wallflowers and give them design power with paint, glazes, metallic leaf, stain, or other creative finishes. You can perk up most materials if you choose the appropriate product and apply it correctly. Use this section to inspire your own surface revivals and to learn techniques that are sure to get the party rolling.

shes

1 MAKING A POINT Paint offers more than color: Paint sheen affects the look and feel of surfaces and entire rooms. The walls of this dining room wear only one color: red. The triangle pattern is created by alternating flat and high-gloss paint of the same color.

2 REFLECTIONS Every room needs a scene-stealer, and this oversize gold-leaf artwork is it. It's pleasing to look at in its own right, and it has the light-reflective qualities of a mirror. The piece helps balance the dramatic features of the room, and casually propped against the wall, it relaxes the formality of the space.

3 IN THE RED Bringing the red paint to the ceiling makes the room seem more intimate. The contrast with the white moldings draws attention to the ceiling coffers.

4 TONED DOWN If a chandelier is too brassy or seems wrong for a room, give it a paint job. Refreshed with a coat of black paint, this chandelier neutralizes the rich reds.

5 TABLE TALK This octagonal table makes for easy dinner conversation and brings shapely interest into the room. The "slices" of wood that form the tabletop are finished in two deep tones for more impact.

6 PLAID PIZZAZZ Plaid draperies introduce pattern and soften the large arched window. Neither too formal nor too casual, plaid works well in almost any setting.

DESIGNED BY **LAURA**

Elegance in Red

Laura polishes the potential of this dining room by trading in neutrals for dramatic color, conventional fleurs-de-lis for jazzy triangles, and excess for streamlined style.

before

This dining room has a lot going for it: thick moldings, an arched window, architecture on the ceiling, and a showy chandelier. The decorating, though, doesn't do any of those extras justice. The stamped fleurs-de-lis on the upper walls are busy and not dramatic enough for the room. Accessories and artwork fail to make a memorable statement. The arched window seems naked without a window treatment. Laura plans to add warmth and drama with color, interesting finishes, and an octagonal table. She also plans to edit the room to create a cleaner look. "Usually on *Trading Spaces*, the challenge is to make a not-so-nice room really nice," she says. "The challenge in this room is to make a nice room really nice."

Though one of the owners of this dining room is an interior designer by trade, she's ready for outside help. "I tried to spruce it up, but it didn't work," she says. Her family agrees that the room—one of the first things visitors see when they step inside the front door—needs some drama to hold its audience.

The owners want classic elegance, and Laura's plan starts traditionally enough: red walls, a mahogany table, and a grand mirrorlike piece. In what turns out to be a series of happy accidents, not all of Laura's ideas pan out.

One case in point is the walls. Laura scraps her plan for cutting custom stencils when it becomes clear that her design is too time-consuming to complete in the designated time frame. After taping off the walls to create guides for Plan B—a series of quick freehand ovals—Laura has an epiphany: The taped-off triangles make a striking design all on their own. The pyramid shapes start above the chair rail and rise to the crown molding; the result is a fashion-forward take

▶ This was one *Trading Spaces* episode when painting over—or rather, staining over—wallpaper was perfectly acceptable. To tone down the grass cloth covering the lower walls, Laura had her team rub stain over it. The darker color brings out the texture and has a rich mahogany tone.

on classic style. On the ceiling, Laura's plan for adding a wash of gold paint over the red is foiled when the gold won't take to the textured surface. However, the high contrast between the red paint and the white moldings is drama enough.

The mahogany table Laura planned to include fails to materialize. Unable to find mahogany wood, Laura plods on with her second choice. She also ends up compromising on her octagonal design when that proves too time-consuming to accomplish before the deadline. Amy Wynn created the table by designing complementary shapes from two types of wood—and joining them with a special joint and brace system on the underside of the table. "It came out really nice through all the evolutionary phases it went through," Laura says. "It's not mahogany, but it's gorgeous."

Gorgeous too is the large gold-leaf piece that mimics a stately mirror. Propped against a wall and flanked by sconces, it's an artsy addition—one of a chosen few. "It was all about editing," Laura says. "Less is more. I didn't want to clutter the walls. By not doing that you see the special pieces."

▶Good editing makes a strong statement. The sculptural centerpiece quietly complements the design of the two-tone table. In the background, a reflective gold-leaf art piece leans on the wall. To create similar artwork, paint a piece of MDF in the desired base coat color, apply gold leaf or another type of metallic leaf, top the board with a clear piece of acrylic, and create a frame from crown molding.

Sheen Scene

Like color choices, paint finishes elicit different responses from different people. Some people like things shiny, and others don't. Here's a look at sheen choices:

▶ **Flat/matte** has virtually no shine to it. It has a good uniform appearance across large areas and is the most forgiving paint for surfaces that aren't perfectly smooth. (Bumps and other flaws on walls are more apparent when coated in paints that reflect light.) It is difficult to clean and therefore best used in low-traffic areas.

▶ **Eggshell** has a bit of shine, without being overly glossy. It resists stains better than flat, so consider it for halls and bathrooms and other low- to medium-traffic areas or for plain trim. (Save shiny coatings for spotlighting special trim and architectural details.)

▶ **Pearl/satin/silk** is a mid-range sheen with a crisp look. It resists dirt and stains and is good for high-traffic areas. The sheen name varies depending on the manufacturer.

▶ **Semigloss** has a noticeable shine to it. It accentuates flaws on any surface because it reflects light. Use it to set off architectural details. It also works well on doors, in hallways, and in children's rooms because it is washable.

▶ **Glossy/high-gloss** is the shiniest of them all. It's durable and easy to wash. It works best for smooth, undamaged surfaces; the higher the gloss, the more it reflects light and reveals imperfections. Use it on moldings, trims, and furniture.

◀ Red is said to stimulate appetite and conversation, so it's a perfect choice for dining rooms. Beware, however: Saturated colors can be difficult to work with, sometimes requiring several coats to achieve a rich, consistent look. Laura splurged on a deep-base tinted primer to minimize the number of coats needed for these walls. For subtle painted pattern, alternate flat paint and high-gloss paint (as Laura did here) when creating your design.

Table On-the-Dot

Visit an office supply store to find what you need for finishing this fun and stylish table.

▶ **MATERIALS**

Old table or new unfinished table

Latex paint in black and white

Low-tack painter's tape

Round color-coding labels in ¾- and ¼-inch sizes

Reinforcement circles

Spray paint in black

▶ **TOOLS**

Sandpaper

Tack cloth

Paintbrushes

Carpenter's square or T square

Pencil

Burnishing tool

Crafts knife

Adhesive remover

Citrus cleanser

Sand the table surface; wipe it clean with a tack cloth. Paint the table base black and the top white; let dry.

Mask off a center panel with low-tack painter's tape (protect the remaining area of the center panel with tape or paper).

Use round color-coding labels and reinforcement circles to mask off "fringe" around the center panel of the tabletop. Use a carpenter's square or a T square to make lightly penciled guidelines for placing the labels (A). Secure labels to the tabletop (B) and burnish them in place.

Spray-paint over the dots; let dry. Remove the labels, using the tip of a crafts knife (C). Let the paint cure for 48 hours. Use an adhesive remover and citrus cleanser to remove any residue left from the stickers.

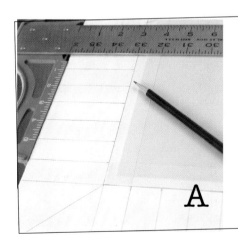
A

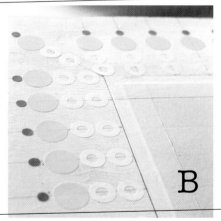
B

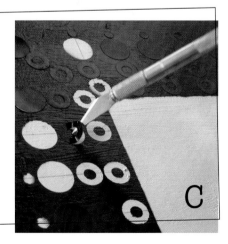
C

◄You'll enjoy seeing dots before your eyes when you apply paint and round office supply stickers to a plain console table. Go dotty!

The Alternate Route... This technique works with any piece of wood furniture. Vary the look by using other sticker shapes or make your own shapes, symbols, letters, or words from adhesive-back shelf-lining paper or frisket film (available at crafts and art supply stores). Experiment with different paint color combinations or use glaze over the adhesive shapes.

Purple
Reign

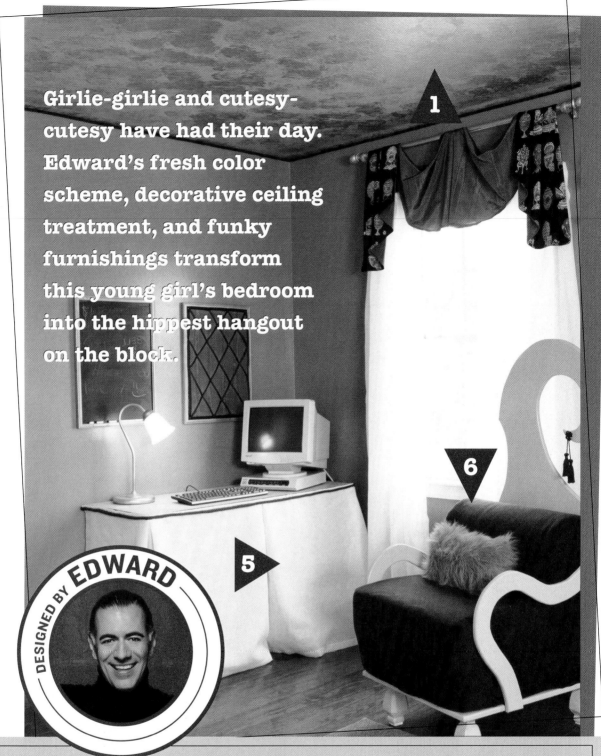

Girlie-girlie and cutesy-cutesy have had their day. Edward's fresh color scheme, decorative ceiling treatment, and funky furnishings transform this young girl's bedroom into the hippest hangout on the block.

DESIGNED BY EDWARD

1 SHINING STAR Flat-painted surfaces are yesterday's news. Here, even the ceiling gets a decorative touch: Silvery paint dabbed on top of a gray hue adds depth and dimension, yielding high drama for a minimal investment of time.

2 STYLISH SIDESHOW Who says a headboard has to go at the head of the bed? With the headboard placed on the long side, this full-size bed takes on the charming look of a daybed. Placing the bed sideways against the window clears space in the center of the room to serve as a kid-friendly hangout. The monogram painted on the headboard makes it clear who reigns here.

3 A GREAT FINISH Dark purple cording finishes the room in style. Easily hot-glued to the top of the wall, it stands in for crown molding and adds definition between the purple walls and the silvery ceiling.

4 FAN FARE Ceiling fans are often ushered out during *Trading Spaces* makeovers. This purple fan, though, is a welcome addition, providing a whirl of color overhead. If you can't find a ceiling fan that coordinates with the color of your room, give an existing fan a fresh coat of paint. (Remove the blades and spray-paint them for a fast, smooth finish; let dry and reinstall.)

5 SKIRTING THE ISSUE Fabric is the great concealer in decorating. Adding a skirt to a table or sink, for example, can hide considerable clutter and extend storage space. No one would ever guess that this desk is pieced together from existing furnishings. Covered with a box-pleated skirt, the desk has the look of a stylish vanity.

6 SAY WHAT? Though its back looks like a big question mark, this chair is unquestionably stylish. The one-of-a-kind design is fun for a child yet fanciful enough to appeal to a preteen—or an older crowd.

before

▶Tallahassee: Ox Bottom Lane

This bedroom has color—and not much else. The bed lacks drama. The furnishings are a mishmash, and a dark sofa seems out of place. The computer desk, a converted vanity, is in the walkway near the bathroom, an awkward location for studying. In addition to giving the room new color and fun style, Edward plans to rearrange the furniture so the center of the room can be used for socializing. The computer will move into the main room, where Edward will fashion a desk from existing furnishings.

◄Within the custom-built frame sits a familiar foldout foam chair. Edward covered it with purple fabric and then elevated it on Amy Wynn's wooden throne, which features fence-post legs and a swirling back. A purple tassel puts an exclamation point on the funky design.

►The swirling motifs painted on the headboard and the shimmering finish of the purple bedspread add visual interest. Painted in a quiet gray tone, the freehand design makes an impact without high contrast.

After bunking with her older sister for three years, the girl who will occupy this space is ready to graduate to her own bedroom. She has high hopes for her new space. "I want it grown-up—something really different than what it is now," she says.

Even the family agrees that something radical is in order. "I want it to be total drama when you walk in—where her friends are just going to want to come over and spend the night," her mom says.

OK, so pink ribbons and bows won't cut it. Edward is up for the challenge, concocting a design that gives the room staying power—it's youthful enough for a "tween," cool enough for a teen, and grown-up enough for a college coed. "And of course, we have to give her some drama," Edward says.

The transformation starts with gray paint. Not exactly dramatic, you say? Wait and see. After giving the ceiling a gray base coat, Edward rags on silver paint to spark the surface to life. (Edward's no-ladder technique involves putting a sponge wrapped in a plastic bag into a long-handled lightbulb changer, dipping it in paint, and dabbing the ceiling.) Silver

►What's a diva without her fur? Fluffy orange trim takes this orange lampshade from so-so to so dramatic. Get out the glue gun and go at it! Fringe and tassel trims also make flirty flourishes for lampshades.

► Paint has an uncanny ability to take on a different look when it's teamed with different elements. The neighbors were initially concerned that the gray paint used on the furnishings and ceiling was too drab. They changed their minds when they saw silver-tone drawer pulls and other silvery accessories draw out the silver tones of the dresser. Fabric sporting Fabergé eggs inspired the colorful artwork.

spray paint transforms accessories into shimmering sensations that offset the brooding battleship gray of the newly painted furnishings.

Though the young occupant had envisioned her room being pale yellow, green, or blue, pastel hues wouldn't yield the drama the family sought. So Edward delivers the punch with purple walls. "To make it fun and youthful, it needed to be just a little bit brighter," he says. "Pale lavender is kind of hard to make funky."

The real funk comes in the accessories. Most notable is the playful curvy chair—more like a contemporary-style throne—built by Amy Wynn. A purple slipcover on the cushions and a tassel dangling from the back add to the regal look. Furry orange pillows and trim make the room fit for a diva, and they are easy enough to swap out down the road. "I love this!" the young occupant says when she sees her new digs. "This is, like, the best!"

◄Featuring a Fabergé egg design, this fabric adds sophistication to the room. The Russian eggs—and their fabric likenesses—are artful and elegant yet colorful and playful enough for a child to appreciate. The window treatment has similar crossover appeal: It looks like a formal, grown-up jabot; however, it's draped in a casual, kid-friendly style. To achieve this look, paint a dowel or a wooden curtain rod with metallic paint, then staple fabric pieces to the wood, letting the fabric drape loosely to create gentle scallops and swoops.

▲This shapely chair perks up what would otherwise be a nondescript vanity. It also shows the importance of sizing up furnishings from the backside when that's how they'll primarily be viewed. The wide black and white stripes are playfully bold and graphic—not too little-girlish, not too serious.

◄A young girl's room needs a bulletin board. Skip the conventional cork and go for something more stylish. Covered in purple fabric, embellished with grosgrain ribbons, and set in a painted frame, this display board fits the overall decor. Mementos, photos of friends, or magazine articles on the latest Hollywood hottie slip between the ribbons for an exhibit that can be changed on a whim.

Paint Pizzazz

Decorative painting techniques continue to be all the rage on walls, on ceilings, on furniture—on almost any surface that can be painted. If wallpapering has lost its appeal, consider one of these decorative paint treatments to banish the blahs:

► **Sponging** has evolved from the high-contrast colors of the '80s to a more blended, sophisticated look. This easy technique involves using a natural sea sponge to dab paint over a wall or ceiling. Choose paints that are similar in color (such as light taupe over dark taupe) or tone (such as medium blue over medium green). If the surface looks too spotty when you're finished, repeat the process to soften the effect.

► **Ragging** includes two techniques: ragging on and ragging off. Ragging on produces a more textured look; ragging off usually produces a subtle, blended look, similar to parchment paper. To rag on, use rags to dab or roll paint or glaze onto a surface. To rag off, dab or blot off still-wet glaze or paint. For either technique, keep plenty of clean rags on hand. Well-worn, lint-free cotton shirts work well. For alternative textures, use crumpled newspaper, plastic grocery bags, or bubble wrap. (For more on rag-rolling, see page 69.)

► **Combing** gives walls a pinstriped look. The technique involves dragging a rubber comb over a wet top coat to remove some of the top coat and expose the base coat color. Use paint as the top coat if you want to emphasize the top color of the treatment; use a tinted-glaze top coat if you want the base color to be more noticeable. It can be difficult to keep the lines straight when combing long stretches of a wall, so this technique may work best below a chair rail.

► **Strié** creates a formal look and the appearance of fabric-covered walls. It involves dragging a stiff-bristle brush through tinted glaze that has been applied over a base coat. (This technique produces thin parallel lines that are less distinct than the pinstripes produced by combing.) Complementary or high-contrast colors—such as green glaze over yellow paint—work best; the stripes are so thin and subtle that low-contrast colors do not have enough impact.

▲ Bold blue and purple squares outlined in crisp white make this space a blockbuster beauty. Stock up on painter's tape and paint rollers and you'll be ready to re-create the look on your own walls.

Color-Block Charisma

Say goodbye to sleepy walls and give a bedroom—or any space in the house—a wake-up call with this graphic grid of painted squares.

Paint on the base coat color, which will later serve as the color for the grid lines; let dry.

Measure the height and the width of the wall to be painted. Decide what size you want the squares to be. (See "Tips for Success" *below*) End squares can be wrapped around the corners of the room, if desired.

Use a colored pencil and measuring tape to mark the desired widths on the wall near the ceiling and floor and at points between. This will ensure straight vertical lines for the squares. Join the marks with a colored pencil and a carpenter's level to ensure accurate, even lines. (Alternatively, snap a chalk line for this process.) Repeat the marking process along

Tips for Success

▶ Use low-tack painter's tape to mask off the blocks and achieve crisp lines. Ordinary masking tape can be difficult to remove and may leave a residue on the wall.

▶ Use your fingernail to burnish the edges of the tape to the wall to prevent the paint from bleeding underneath.

▶ When determining the sizes of the squares, allow for the width of the grid lines. For example, if you want 22-inch squares with a 1-inch-wide grid line between squares, figure the grid into your planning and measuring.

▶ Whenever possible, remove painter's tape before the paint dries to avoid pulling up paint.

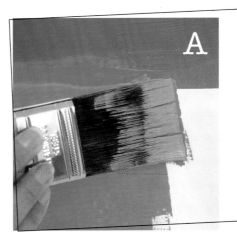

the height of the wall to establish the horizontal lines of the squares.

Using painter's tape, mask off the squares, using the predetermined marks (the width of the tape will be the grid width). Tape an X inside the squares not being painted

with the first block color (so you won't accidentally paint them the wrong color). Paint the masked-off squares with the first color. Remove the Xs from the remaining squares and paint them with the second color (A). Remove the tape to reveal the base coat color (B) and let dry.

Shipshape Living Room

1 BLOCK PARTY Even inexpensive drop ceilings with pop-out tiles can withstand paint and make a fashion statement in their own right. Wearing the same dynamic color-block outfit as the walls, this ceiling "pops" with style.

2 CUSHY JOB Attention to detail perfects a room. These new blue cushions connect with the blue rectangles. Adding a cushion or re-covering an existing one is a quick and easy way to unify furnishings within a new color scheme.

3 SHELF HELP Hung on the wall, this bookcase serves as a display space and echoes the shape of the painted blocks. Coated with the same black paint as the desk below, the bookcase takes on the look of a hutch.

4 LAUNCHING PAD Design inspiration comes in many forms. This tray with matching cups and saucers inspired the paint treatment.

5 LOWRIDERS Low-slung furnishings can visually heighten a ceiling. Cutting off the legs of these ottomans and matching wicker furnishings maximizes the sense of headroom on the houseboat.

6 CLEVER COVER-UP If a room has an unsightly feature, building around it is sometimes a smart approach—and less costly than other options. This bar camouflages the inoperative navigation wheel of the houseboat.

7 SOFT TOUCH Roman shades can be crisp and tailored, falling into tidy folds when raised. Or they can be unstructured like these shades. The casual look of these window treatments befits the laid-back lifestyle on the houseboat. The soft folds and gentle curves offer contrast to the color-block walls and ceiling.

DESIGNED BY **HILDI**

The owners of this houseboat worked hard to turn the dated main room into a neutral space that they could begin to redecorate. To enliven the room, Hildi lets loose with a color-block treatment in eight colors.

The owners gave up living on land nearly three years ago in favor of a houseboat moored at a marina. The fact that their boat doesn't have a motor and can't sail the seas doesn't bother them. "We're not really sailing people," one owner says. "We just like to live on the water. It's a very laid-back lifestyle."

Their wicker furniture fit the casual lifestyle; however, all else on the houseboat failed to satisfy their eye for style. They tore out dated carpeting and refreshed the walls with new beige paint, essentially turning their living room into a blank canvas so they could start anew. The question was, Where to start? They knew they wanted color (though not red), and one owner, especially, longed for a tropical Jimmy Buffett-style getaway complete with a tiki bar.

Hildi nixes the tropical idea and opts for a multicolor paint treatment that has staying power. The color-block treatment, with its eight-color palette, is a lofty goal for a two-day project. After marking off and painting wide stripes in the different colors, the team rolls on random color blocks. The technique rises to the ceiling, where foam tiles get an invigorating update.

◄This end table and its mate on the other end of the sofa are the only pieces of furniture Hildi brought into the room. The stain and white top echo the brown and white in the color-block treatment on the walls, ceiling, and bar. The lamp and vase offer shapely contrast to the rectangles.

before

▶Tampa/St. Pete: Harborage Marina

Except for an occasional blip of color—namely, a pillow and an area rug—this living room is bland. The furniture arrangement functions at a less than optimal level. The wheel of the houseboat is unsightly—especially given the fact that this is a year-round home that never leaves the marina and therefore doesn't need a wheel. Hildi plans to give the room a bold color-block treatment, rearrange the furniture, and cover the wheel by turning the area into a bar.

►Tricked out with a mod geometric design, this bar is a seaworthy addition to the room: It's built from teak found at a boat salvage yard. The top of the center section lifts to reveal the navigation wheel. The end section has shelves built into it to hold glassware and other items.

▼When the sun sets, the Roman shades can be pulled down and the candles in these silvery candelabra lit to create an intimate evening on the water. Because Hildi used most of the owners' existing furnishings, she was able to devote a good portion of her budget to all-important accessories—in this case, candles, lamps, and more.

◄Pillow fabrics repeat the linear and rectangular motif that dominates the room. The quiet colors of the fabrics keep the look subtle.

A new salvaged-teak bar hides the unused steering device. It's built in sections for easy mobility in case the owners decide to add a motor someday. Painted with the color-block treatment, the bar provides a focal point at the end of the room.

Hildi's energized paint treatment is only her first bold move. To give the ceiling the illusion of height, she chops off the legs on the owners' wicker furnishings. She also turns the tables on the furniture arrangement: The TV and dining table, for example, move to positions nearly opposite their original locations. The wicker

▼Hildi purchased this plastic tray and matching cups and saucers in Paris; this charming set served as the inspiration point around which to design this room.

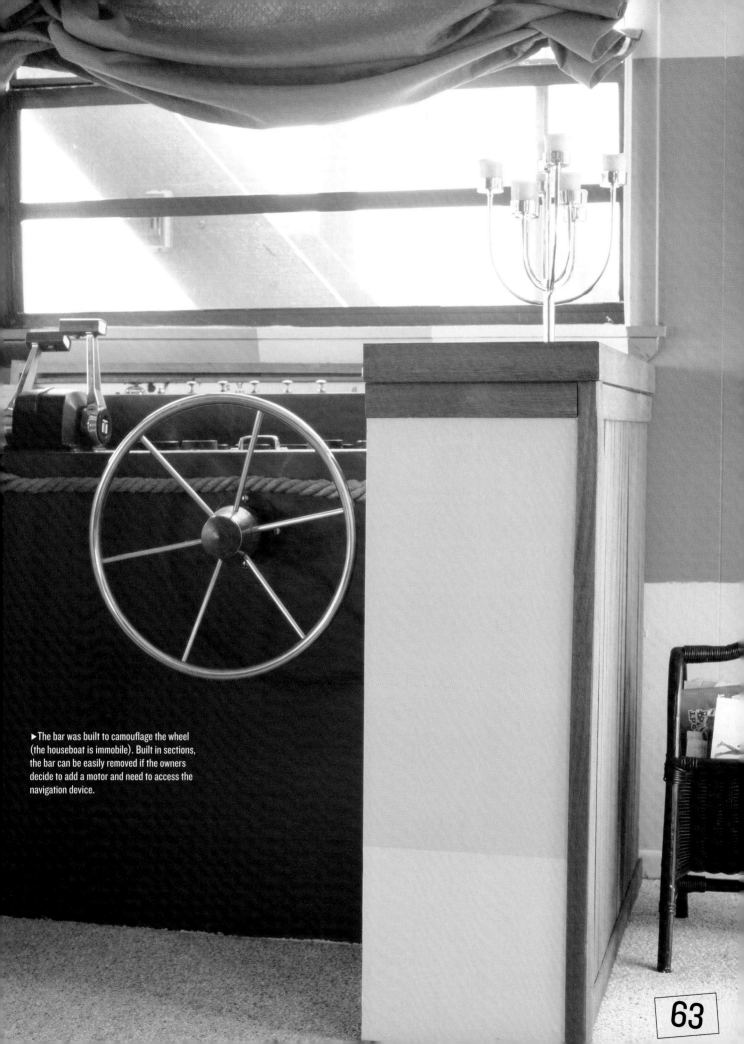

▶The bar was built to camouflage the wheel (the houseboat is immobile). Built in sections, the bar can be easily removed if the owners decide to add a motor and need to access the navigation device.

furniture huddles near the center of the room in an intimate conversation grouping. "It's amazing how much room we have now," one owner says. "It's the same amount of things; it's just the distribution of them that makes all the difference in the world."

The room isn't the tropical paradise one owner had hoped for, yet after taking it all in, the owners agree that they have gained their main wishes: color, more space, and a bar. "Even though it was different than we expected, Hildi actually gave us what we were asking for," one owner says.

Color Schemes

Whether ready-made or custom-blended, paint color options are virtually limitless. But, choosing colors that work well together can be daunting. If you're planning a multicolor paint scheme, consider these options:

▶ **Choose neighborly hues.** Start with a favorite color, then look on either side of it on the color wheel. If you like both of the colors, include them in your scheme. If you only like one of the colors, select that one and use the color next to it as a third hue.

▶ **Go monochromatic.** For a monochromatic scheme, use only one color and vary the shades for interest. Even a neutral color like beige comes in many shades—from darker browns to sandy taupes to creamy caramels.

▶ **Keep it cool—or warm.** Pull together a palette by combining either all cool colors or all warm colors. Draw a line through a color wheel to determine what colors fall in each category. On one side you'll see cool blues, greens, and violets. On the other side are warm reds, oranges, and yellows.

▶ **Consider intensity.** Color intensity is as important as the colors themselves. Paint chips are usually arranged with the lightest tone at the top and the darkest at the bottom. To choose colors that have equal intensities, select the third color down on each paint chip, for example. Alternatively, use the ready-made palette paint cards that many stores now offer, which put together a coordinated color scheme for you.

▲Painted black and hung on the wall, this bookcase is an ideal display shelf. Hildi retrofitted the bookcase so one shelf accommodates figurines collected by one of the owners while he was in the Navy. She also left a reminder of herself: a palette of the colors used in the room.

◀These abstract paintings repeat the rectangular motif; the colors are subtle so they harmonize with the walls. For each of the paintings, Hildi mixed a color used in the room with white paint and painted stripes down an artist's canvas until she achieved the desired look. Slim downlights illuminate the artwork.

▼Hildi is known for her daring design, and she took daring to new heights on the owners' wicker furnishings. She cut off the legs to make the low ceiling seem higher, leaving enough leg on the chairs to ensure comfort. Black paint gives the grouping a new attitude—and visual weight that can stand up to the busy walls.

▲The imperfections that naturally occur as you stamp a design on your custom tablecloth give the piece character and charm. If you must touch up a spot or two, use either a scrap of foam to stamp on the paint or dab a bit of paint onto the cloth with a small, flat, stiff brush.

Perk Up Plain Fabric

Walls, floors, and furniture have been wearing paint for years. Now fabric can play dress-up too. A plain tablecloth takes on new personality and any color palette you choose when you decorate the material with this stamping technique.

Wash and dry the tablecloth; iron. Plan your design on paper, cutting out shapes and experimenting with placement (A). Figure dimensions so the pattern will fit evenly along the edges of the tablecloth. (If your tablecloth is round or oval, fold the cloth in half and measure one curved side with a fabric tape measure. Multiply this measurement by 2 to determine how much space is available along the edge.)

Parallel to the hem, mark off guidelines for stamping, using the disappearing-ink pen.

Use a purchased stamp or cut the stamp shapes from the rubber stamp surface, using a crafts knife (B) or sharp scissors. Use superstrong glue to affix the cut stamp to a wood scrap or clear acrylic. Clear acrylic works well because it lets you see exactly where you are aligning the stamp (C).

Make a stamp pad by spreading acrylic paint on the foam sheet or on paper toweling on a disposable plate. Use a plastic spreader to spread the paint on the pad.

Spread out the tablecloth and find the center point of one edge. (Fold a round or oval tablecloth in half and find the center point along the curved edge.) Working on a padded surface, begin stamping at the center of one edge, working to each corner (or to the fold line on a round or oval cloth). Stamp opposite sides and let dry before stamping the other two sides. Adjust the pattern if the design isn't coming out evenly.

▶ **MATERIALS**
Paper
Purchased tablecloth, 100 percent cotton
Scraps of wood or clear acrylic
Acrylic paint
Thin sheet of craft foam or pad of paper towels on a disposable plate (for stamp pad)

▶ **TOOLS**
Iron and ironing board
Crafts knife or sharp scissors
Fabric tape measure
Disappearing-ink pen
Blank rubber stamp surface (to make your own stamp) or a purchased stamp
Superstrong glue
Plastic spreader

A

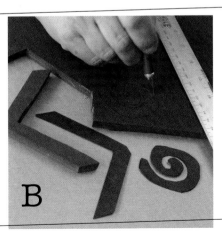

B

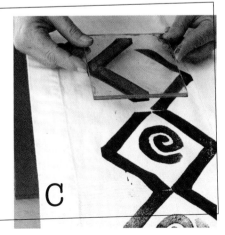

C

67

Facts for Fabulous Finishes

Paint and stain are two affordable mediums that *Trading Spaces* crews often use to give walls and furniture fresh color and flair. Check out these products and projects and use them to enliven your own rooms.

Prep Talk

Preparing the surfaces to be painted or stained and protecting the surrounding areas are essential steps on the path to a successful finish. When painting or staining wood, lightly sand surfaces smooth and wipe away residue with a tack cloth. Fill holes in walls with spackling compound; fill dents and holes in wood surfaces with stainable/paintable wood filler. Let fillers dry. Sand lightly and wipe away residue with a tack cloth.

To protect surrounding surfaces that you don't want to paint or stain, such as molding or window trim, use a low-tack quick-release tape, such as those shown *below*, and newspaper or other large paper sheets as needed. Though painter's tape is more expensive than regular masking tape, it comes up cleanly, leaving no residue. If desired, tape drop cloths or newspaper to the base moldings to keep paint or stain from splattering on the floor. Remove furnishings or cover furniture pieces with drop cloths.

Whenever possible, remove painter's tape before the paint dries to reduce the possibility of pulling up paint. One exception is when you are painting an entire room and you know you will need to apply more than one coat. If reapplying tape and newspapers would be too time-consuming, leave them in place until you finish painting the final coat; then remove the tape. If you pull up any paint, go back and touch up those spots later.

Tips for Success

CEILING FIRST

If you are planning to paint the ceiling, paint it before the walls. Use a 2 ½- or 3-inch angled-bristle brush to outline the ceiling. This technique is known as "cutting in." Paint the ceiling with a roller mounted on an extension handle to avoid standing on a ladder.

You also need to cut in all walls, including around moldings, where walls meet, and where walls meet the ceiling. Use an angled-bristle brush to ensure a clean edge in areas that may be difficult to reach with a roller.

◀ Apply painter's tape when you want to create crisp edges, for example, when you paint stripes on walls or stain geometric shapes on furniture.

Rags to Riches

Create beautiful walls by ragging paint on or off a dry base coat. Start with a mixture of 4 parts glaze to I part paint. Roll up an old cotton T-shirt (and keep extras handy) and follow these steps:

▲ To create the ragged-on effect *above,* dip a damp rolled rag into the glaze mixture and roll the cloth across the surface using light pressure. Allow some of the base coat color to show through. Repeat the process to cover the wall.

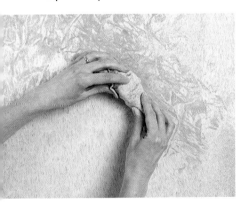

▲ For a slightly different look, use the ragging-off technique *above.* Start by rolling the glaze mixture onto a 4-foot section of the wall. Roll the cloth onto the wall, pouncing and wiping it to remove some of the glaze mixture and expose some of the base coat. Reposition and turn the rag to avoid repeating the pattern. Repeat the process in 4×4-foot sections to finish the wall. To avoid smudged corners, let each wall dry before continuing to the next wall.

Paint Harlequin Diamonds

A classic painted harlequin diamond pattern remains a perennial favorite for dressing up walls and other surfaces. Paint a base coat of the lightest diamond color and let dry. Then follow these steps, working with a partner:

1) After determining what size you want the diamonds to be, start at an upper corner of the wall where it meets the ceiling and measure half of the width of the diamond design (in this example, 2 inches). Make a mark with a colored pencil that matches the darker diamond color. After that mark, measure the full width of the diamond design (in this example, 4 inches) and mark accordingly. Continue marking diamond widths to the end of the wall.

2) Return to the upper corner where you began. Measure down half the height of the diamond design (in this example, 3 inches). Make a mark with a colored pencil. After that mark, measure the full height of the diamond design (in this example, 6 inches) and mark it on the wall. Continue marking diamond heights down the end of the wall.

3) Working with a partner, connect the marks diagonally with chalk lines to form the diamond design.

4) For crisp diamonds, use painter's tape to mask off the lines and tape an X within each diamond not to be painted. For a freehand look, skip the painter's tape. Paint every other diamond with the top coat color and let dry.

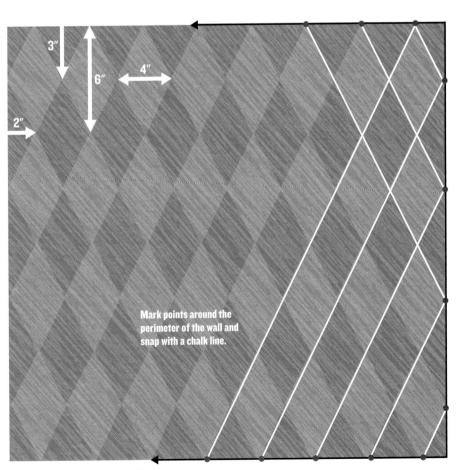

Mark points around the perimeter of the wall and snap with a chalk line.

▲ Harlequin Diamonds pattern

Stain Starters

Visit the stain aisle of any home center to see your options—hundreds of products for finishing wood surfaces. Wood conditioners can be used to prepare some softwoods to receive stain more evenly. Water-base stains are popular because they dry faster than oil-base stains and give off less odor. However, they can be difficult to apply evenly over large areas. Oil-base stains usually provide a richer finish. You'll also find gels (which don't run, drip, or splash), dyes (which offer deep, unusual colors such as red, blue, orange, green, and black), and stain pens (for easily touching up scratches in stain finishes).

Apply stain with a synthetic- or natural-bristle brush or a disposable foam brush; wipe off the layer of finish with clean rags. When the surface is dry, apply a second coat to deepen the color, if desired. Wear rubber gloves to avoid discoloring your fingers. Protect the surface by applying a sealer, such as one of the products shown *opposite*.

Brush and Roller Basics

Choose a variety of quality paintbrushes for your finishing projects. For basic painting, you'll need good-quality synthetic- or nylon-bristle brushes with flat and angled bristles. Flat-bristle brushes work for general painting; angled- or tapered-bristle brushes are great for trim.

Use only synthetic-bristle brushes with latex (water-base) paint. Natural-hair bristles will frizz if exposed to water-base products. Natural- or synthetic-bristle brushes will

work for alkyd paint or oil-base stain; natural bristles provide a better finish. After cleaning, store brushes in their original protective plastic covers to help the bristles maintain their shape.

Rollers and roller covers come in different sizes to suit various projects. When selecting a roller cover, consider the surface you'll be painting: A short-nap roller works best on smooth surfaces, while long-nap rollers are perfect for rough surfaces. To test the

quality of your chosen roller cover, squeeze it. A quality cover will quickly return to its original shape. Separate the nap on the roller cover—if you see the cardboard core, the nap may not be dense enough to deliver a smooth coat of paint. Use synthetic roller covers for water-base products and synthetic or natural-fiber covers for oil-base products.

Clear Coats

After painting or staining wood furniture, protect the finish. The look you want and the level of protection the piece requires will dictate your choice of finishes. Read the label to determine the best method of application—brush, sponge applicator, or sprayer. Some manufacturers recommend that you lightly sand the second-to-last coat after it dries to ensure a smooth finish.

Protect painted finishes. Flat, eggshell, and satin paint finishes can be protected with poly-acrylic (which is water-base) or polyurethane (which is available in both water- and oil-base formulas). Semigloss and gloss paint finishes offer water resistance and don't accept clear finishes well.

Preserve character. If you want to achieve a matte-antique look, for example, a wax or linseed/teak oil finish is a good choice. Neither, however, will protect the surface from moisture damage.

Resist heat. If your finish needs to stand up to heat, oil-base polyurethane is an excellent choice. Varnish and Danish oil provide good heat resistance.

Save time. Some products on the market provide stain and polyurethane in one step, so you save application time. These combination products also allow you to change the stain color of a previously finished piece without removing the old finish.

Repel water. Shellac, lacquer, varnish, poly-acrylic, and polyurethane all do a good job of repelling water. Danish oil does a fair job.

To the Finish

Some of the most memorable jaw-dropping moments on *Trading Spaces* happen during the Paint Reveal segment. This review of finish favorites illustrates that the designers rarely choose the ordinary.

1 DESIGNED BY DOUG

2 DESIGNED BY GENEVIEVE

3 DESIGNED BY VERN

1 CAPTURE TRANQUILLITY Randomly crosshatching three shades of blue glaze onto walls base-coated in blue yields a cloudlike, ethereal bedroom in California: Dusty Trail. Doug paints the dark cherry wood furnishings white to draw them into the scheme. He then rubs on a dark glaze that makes the pieces appear aged. Even the hardware on the furniture receives a new finish—hammered-pewter spray paint.

2 CHALK ONE UP By coating the walls with sage green chalkboard paint, Gen plays up a French butcher shop theme for this kitchen in California: Dusty Trail. Applied over a coat of tinted primer, chalkboard paint mimics the familiar classroom surface and actually functions like the real thing. The smooth painted finish wipes clean with a chalkboard eraser or a soft damp cloth.

3 STRIPE IT RICH High ceilings make new and old houses seem grand. However, the same soaring heights that wow in the living room can feel unfriendly in the bedroom. In Indiana: Fieldhurst Lane, Vern makes the bedroom more intimate and contemporary by painting horizontal wall stripes that ground the space.

4 ADD VINTAGE FLAIR The finish you choose for the background in your room can complement belongings as well as the house. In Pittsburgh: Penn Avenue, Christi enhances the charm of the 130-year-old house and creates a nicely textured foil for antique tin tiles when she applies joint compound to all the walls. Red paint—toned down later with walnut stain— elegantly plays up the antique feel of the room.

5 SHAPE YOUR FUTURE If a room lacks architectural interest, adapt this faux-parchment technique used by Doug in Minneapolis: IIth Avenue. Randomly tape off blocks and dab on ivory and tan paint to create a look as regal and substantial as the stone walls of a castle.

6 SHINE ON Vern shows how to make a ceiling sophisticated in Pennsylvania: Tremont Drive. Layering on copper leaf one piece at a time was tedious. However, the striking results are a permanent reward.

Chapter Three

Archit

Flat notes have a place in musical scores, but not in well-designed rooms. Unadorned, boxy interiors can make your whole house seem out of tune. This section sings praises to all the elements that can make a space more grand and, well, notable. You'll learn how the *Trading Spaces* crew spiffs up ordinary spaces with clever architectural tricks. You'll also find some projects and insider tips that will help you compose your own architectural arias.

ectural Details
That Sing

Relaxed Retreat

2

4

1

3

Despite periodic efforts, the owners of this bedroom couldn't quite create the relaxing getaway they pictured in their dreams. Frank comes to the rescue and gives them a quiet refuge that is both classy and quaint.

DESIGNED BY FRANK

1 PANEL DISCUSSION The beaded-board wainscoting gobbles up a good slice of the budget yet gives the room much-needed architectural oomph. Painting the panels white makes the space feel like a romantic cottage getaway.

2 LOOKING UP Paint can enhance or diminish architectural features. Here it's all about enhancement: The newly painted tray ceiling, a lovely shade of brown, now commands attention.

3 WOVEN WONDER Assign your furnishings extra work. This custom chair pulls double duty as a coatrack yet refuses to compromise on style. With its textural basket-weave design, it's the focal point of the wall.

4 MAKE A CONNECTION There's something to be said for understatement. Though flowing side panels would have been a style-appropriate choice for this room, this roll-up shade is a clean and clever alternative. The shade spans most of the width of the wall to connect two windows. Rolled up, it functions as a cornice to bring more architectural character to this side of the room.

5 BLISSFUL SLUMBER Banish conflict from the bedroom by choosing bed linens that are appropriate for your bed. This four-poster featuring sumptuous swirls wears a deep regal red. The bedding is stylish without stealing the show.

6 AGING GRACEFULLY An intriguing aged patina is yours for the asking—or the doing. Frank gives this artwork old-world flair by using joint compound for texture, adhering a small architectural element, and applying stain.

▲Playing up the ornamentation on the existing headboard, where leaves flow out from the center, small tassels seem to grow out of the large tassel adorning this pillow. Placing the pillow in the center draws the eye to the headboard detail.

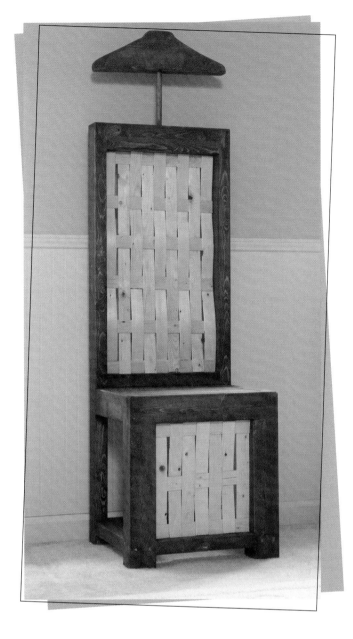

The owners invested in a stately four-poster for their master bedroom, thinking their room design would fall into place from there. They worked on the bedroom in fits and spurts after long days at work; still, it wasn't the warm and inviting retreat they knew it could be. "It's got a lot of potential," one owner says.

Frank concurs. He's rarely given a room with nice proportions, architectural details—including crown molding and a deep tray ceiling—and good furniture, yet this room has it all. Ultimately, the bed does cue the room design. Noting its rich wood tones and traditional look, Frank says, "I'm seeing old-world inn with all this heavy furniture."

The transformation begins with a three-color paint scheme of milky white, sandy beige, and mocha brown. Frank's thoughtful paint placement draws out the best features of the room. Painted brown, the tray ceiling gains impact. The dark wood furnishings pop against the white-painted wainscoting, making this

▲It's a chair. It's a hanger. It's a ... silent butler. Or at least that's what Frank calls this handy helper inspired by hotel furnishings. The hanger can hold a suit jacket or other garments. The seat provides a place for putting on socks and shoes or stacking tomorrow's outfit. Basket-weave inlays take the piece from functional to sculptural.

▶Consider texture an architectural element. To create a base for old-world wall art, apply joint compound to a canvas or paper and then roll and unroll it to create wrinkles and cracks. Frank's wall hangings look like the plastered wallpapers of yesteryear.

▶**Atlanta: Highlands Trace**

This master bedroom has potential yet needs a designer's touch to make it something special. The stark white bed linens are at odds with the elegant and traditional four-poster. The walls lack color and artwork. Frank plans to give the room old-world elegance via luxurious bedding and custom artwork. Then he'll dress up the walls with wainscoting and a chair rail. Soothing colors will help the room relax.

Know the Lingo

If you don't know wainscoting from dentil molding, read on. This list will help you come to terms with common architectural details:

▶ **Wainscoting** refers to wood panels adhered over walls. It usually covers one-third or two-thirds of the lower wall. Wainscoting may feature panels (for a formal look) or molding strips (for a Craftsman-style board-and-batten treatment). The panels can be painted or stained. A chair rail usually finishes the top of the panels. Tile or marble also can be used as wainscoting.

▶ **Beaded board** (a term sometimes used interchangeably with wainscoting) features slats of wood adhered side by side. It's now widely available in sheets, with tiny grooves that give the appearance of individual slats; using sheets makes the installation easier. Beaded board is a hallmark of casual cottage style. It can cover lower walls, march all the way up to a ceiling, or even cover a ceiling.

▶ **Chair rail** is a strip of molding applied horizontally on walls, usually about 30 to 36 inches above the floor. Although a chair rail is often used to finish the top of wainscoting, it can be used alone for a visual break between paint colors, wallcoverings, and other coverings or finishes. Chair rails are often purely decorative. However, they had a practical original purpose: to prevent the backs of chairs from rubbing against and damaging walls.

▶ **Crown molding** is a popular traditional trim installed at the top of a wall, where the wall meets the ceiling. Crown moldings can be deep and showy, or narrow and plain. Corners are mitered to ensure a proper fit.

▶ **Dentil molding** is a type of trim that features closely spaced rectangular blocks. It is often teamed with other types of molding to add a decorative flourish. Dentil molding works well with many design styles.

▶ **Picture rail** is adhered high on a wall—from a few inches to a foot below the ceiling. Though it now serves mainly as decoration, it was originally used to suspend artwork so that walls would not be damaged with nail holes.

▶ **Baseboard** is a molding strip installed at the bottom of a wall. On uncarpeted floors, a narrow, rounded strip of wood called quarter round is usually added along the bottom edge of the baseboard.

▲This originally clear glass plate lived a closet existence inside a cupboard until Frank turned it into a display piece. Handmade papers torn in different shapes and sizes create the artful collage. The papers are adhered to the back of the plate with decoupage medium, giving the illusion of handcrafted pottery.

newest architectural addition worth the investment in time and money. The beige on the upper walls eases the transition between the light and dark colors, swathing the room in serenity.

Frank applies old-world textures to custom artwork to take the visual interest up another notch. He relies on two common building materials—joint compound and stain—to create wall hangings, which have the look of aged leather or an old plaster wallcovering. A two-tone wooden chair with soldier-straight angles is a welcome contemporary addition to the generally traditional scheme.

What about the bed? Dressed in an opulent bedspread and plumped with pillows, it revels in regality. The owners pronounce it gorgeous, and now, with their design worries gone, they can sleep easy.

▶ Like the wall and ceiling treatment, which graduates from light to dark, this chair is a study in contrasts. The dark stain unites the piece with the existing wood furnishings, while the lighter portions give the piece modern appeal. Ty created the basket-weave detailing by weaving planed strips of 2×4s.

▼ A garden center is a great place to shop for decorative accents, especially if your room has earthy undertones or needs a boost of texture. Brought inside, this twiggy structure slips over an inexpensive cylinder lamp, adding intrigue and a focal point that towers like the bedposts. Embellished with decorative paper, the formerly white lamp casts a golden glow in the room; such an embellishment is advisable only if a lamp uses a low-wattage bulb.

Molding Magic

Create the illusion of substantial crown and base moldings by combining paint and low-cost narrow moldings with existing woodwork.

Paint the existing crown and base moldings white; let dry. Measuring down 5 inches from the bottom of the crown molding, use a pencil and a carpenter's level to make a horizontal guideline around the perimeter of the room. Make a second horizontal guideline 5 inches above the base molding. Mask off the guidelines, using low-tack painter's tape, and paint the area between the guidelines and the existing moldings white (A).

Remove the tape; let dry.

Use a circular saw or a miter box and backsaw to cut 1¼-inch-wide moldings to the desired lengths and position them over the edges of the newly painted bands. Use finishing nails and a hammer to secure moldings (B).

Cut vertical battens to length and nail to the wall between the top (C) and bottom molding embellishments. Space battens about 18 inches apart.

▶ **MATERIALS**
White paint
Low-tack painter's tape
1¼-inch-wide molding of your choice (to enhance existing crown and base moldings)
Finishing nails
1⅝-inch-wide low-profile batten-style moldings (for vertical embellishments)

▶ **TOOLS**
Paintbrush
Measuring tape
Pencil
Carpenter's level
Circular saw or a miter box and a backsaw
Hammer

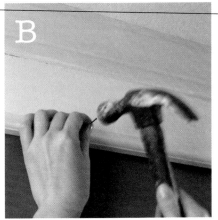

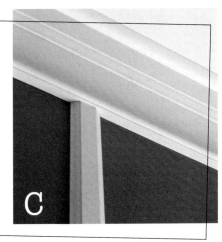

◄ Painting moldings crisp white and installing them on a background of bold color makes a dramatic statement, as illustrated by this classic blue and white scheme. Paint the wall the desired background color before adding molding embellishments.

Tips for Molding

Before applying new moldings to walls, paint them the desired color and let dry. Once the moldings are secured with finishing nails, fill nail holes with wood filler, let the filler dry, and touch up the filled spots with matching paint.

If you plan to add vertical batten-style moldings to your walls, as shown here, select crown and base molding embellishments that are wide enough to accommodate the tops and bottoms of the battens. See photograph C.

1

3

4

2

Fresh-Start
Kitchen

1 HIGH-RISING DRAMA Unexpected touches make a room sparkle with style. This fancy chandelier—something more commonly found in a formal dining room—veers the kitchen toward the elegant side.

2 SHAPING UP Count on slipcovers to keep your secrets. Batting placed over the back and seat of a $20 unfinished wooden chair creates the look of a tailored parsons chair. A linen slipcover keeps the truth under wraps.

3 FLOWER POWER With their satiny texture and sensuous lines, these calla lilies add instant glamour. The white-on-white scheme is sleek and streamlined.

4 GATHER ROUND If you have it, flaunt it. With a curvy pedestal and a stencil-enhanced top, this stylish table has no reason to cover up with a tablecloth. The table suits the space much better than the rectangular one that was previously in the room.

5 COOL COMBO Color is the most noticeable element in decorating, and if you let loose with it, you'll create amazing atmosphere. Lavender walls offer high contrast to the white molding so the new architectural details stand out.

6 NEW DEPTH Molding strips bring architectural character and dimension to a lackluster wall, creating the look of a classic paneled room. The treatment also balances the tall cabinetry on the other side of the room.

DESIGNED BY **RICK**

It's out with the old (beige and boring) and in with the new (color and architectural character) for this kitchen. Rick's glamorous design is a feast for the eyes.

▶White can make a room feel more spacious, yet too much white can be glaring. White cabinetry can stay if you opt for a "white plus one" color scheme. For the most part, in this kitchen whatever isn't white is lavender. Repeating the two colors creates easy flow from the workspace to the eating area. White paint coats the oak trim around the countertops and the terra-cotta pots on the cupboards, streamlining the look even more. A few touches of black, such as the new cabinet hardware, ground the scheme.

◀Stenciled designs that echo the curves of the table legs march around the tabletop and draw the eye to the elegant centerpiece. Rick wanted the black stenciling to look slightly aged, so he used a pouncing motion with a paintbrush to let some of the white show through. Other ways to age or tone down a stenciled motif include rubbing the design with steel wool or glazing or whitewashing the surface.

▼This rectangular table features a pedestal that matches the dining table design. It functions as a stylish study desk for the owner's children.

This kitchen had served its owner well as a hardworking hub. It was a place to gather for family dinners, a homework station for the owner's two children, and a lounge where everyone could hang out. The only missing ingredient—and a big one at that—was style. "Since they spend so much time in there, it would be nice if it were really just upbeat and fun and maybe kind of different," says a relative who signed on to help with the room redo.

Wanting to give the family a pick-me-up after the loss of their husband and father, Rick kicks out the blahs with a refreshing approach to kitchen design. He plans to grace the room with a combination of Hollywood glam and Art Deco streamlining while leaving everyday convenience intact. "I have one word and one word only in my vocabulary, and that is 'elegance,'" he says.

before

▶Alabama: Mallard Lake Drive

This kitchen has a functional workspace, white cabinetry, and an eat-in dining area. However, the room lacks drama and is crowded, even a bit cluttered. The table outside the work core is too large for the space, and its rectangular shape looks dull and clumsy in this setting. A freestanding cabinet takes up even more space in the dining area. Rick plans to infuse the room with color, streamline the space, and add architectural detail.

◄With its thick curves, the pedestal design commands attention. Carter cut the table base from pieces of MDF and then nailed them together.

Rick begins the makeover with color. Bright white teams with an elegant hue that dances between lavender and blue. Used lavishly, the colors work in tandem to unify and streamline the space. Touches of black have a grounding effect.

Dispensing with artwork and pattern, Rick creates interest with moldings that mimic classic wall panels. Painted glossy white, the moldings pop against the lavender walls. Two new tables, also painted white, move beyond utilitarian to sculptural with curvy pedestal bases and detailed tops.

The room achieves a state of grace with a nine-light chandelier. The fixture, crystals, and shades cost $410, and Rick admits that such a purchase "goes against all *Trading Spaces* logic." Still, it establishes the room as a culinary classic.

"I think it's a very fresh place," Rick says. "I think it's a very appetizing place."

▲This black and white chandelier makes a graphic statement. Rick spray-painted the wrought-iron fixture white and the crystals black to set the piece apart from ordinary chandeliers. Black lampshades add visual weight.

Defining Style

While design trends come and go, elegance always stays in style. Here are four popular enduring styles that designers use to give rooms grace and timeless good looks:

▸ **Classical** style became popular in the 15th and 16th centuries, revived by the Renaissance. Its characteristics include proportion and Greek and Roman motifs, such as urns, scrolls, acanthus leaves, and wreaths.

▸ **Neoclassic** style blossomed in the 1700s and is considered the first real international style. It derives from classical style and developed as a reaction against the highly elaborate rococo style. Restraint, symmetry, and proportion are hallmarks of neoclassic style. Classical motifs, such as acanthus leaves and lion heads, are decorative elements.

▸ **Art Nouveau** was the forerunner of Art Deco. This style first became popular between 1890 and 1910. It is characterized by flowing lines, sinuous curves, and stylized forms derived from nature.

▸ **Art Deco** is a style of architecture and furnishings that was first popular in the 1920s and 1930s. Characteristics include streamlined, geometric motifs and the use of materials such as glass, plastic, and chrome.

▼With the addition of custom-cut moldings, a plain armoire can look contemporary, funky, casual, or traditional. Here mirrors and moldings laid on the bias make this crisp, white armoire an elegant focal point in a casual family room.

▶ MATERIALS

Armoire with plain doors

Mirror squares, 2 (5 ½×5 ½ inches)

Mirror mastic

Beaded tongue-and-groove paneling (⁵⁄₁₆×4 inches)

Brads or short finishing nails

½-inch molding

White paint

▶ TOOLS

Sawhorses or large worktable

Tape measure

Pencil

Straightedge

Circular saw or miter box and backsaw

Coping saw

Paintbrushes

Jazzy-Door Armoire

Give a plain armoire pizzazz by adding moldings and mirrors to the doors.

Remove the doors and lay them flat across sawhorses or on a large worktable. Around the perimeter of each door front, mark 1½-inch-wide borders with a pencil and straightedge.

it as a diamond shape so that the corners of the mirror align with the penciled lines (A). Secure the mirror with mirror mastic. Repeat for the second door.

Using a miter box and a backsaw

Frame each panel with ⅛-inch molding cut with mitered corners (C). Paint the doors and the armoire body white; let dry and reattach the doors.

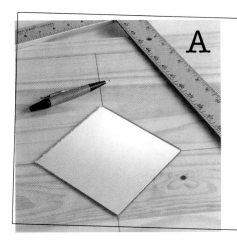 A

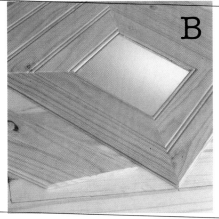 B

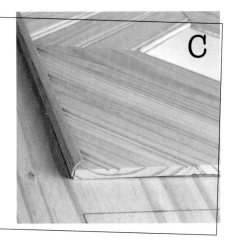 C

Mark locations for the three raised panels on each door, leaving 1½ inches between each panel. Note: On these doors, the top panels measure 9 inches high, the center panels are 17 inches square, and the bottom panels are 30 inches high.

Find the center of the center panel; use a pencil and straightedge to mark a horizontal and a vertical line within the center panel so the lines intersect at this center point. Center a mirror on top of the intersecting lines and position

or a circular saw set at a 45-degree angle, cut the paneling to fit around the mirror and inside the penciled border of the square. Use a coping saw to remove the tongue edge that meets the mirror. Secure paneling to the door with brads or small finishing nails. Repeat for the second door.

Mark vertical lines at the center of each remaining panel. Use the vertical lines as guides for laying out pieces of paneling. Cut at a 45-degree angle at each end, the pieces will lie side by side to form the angular bias design (B).

The Alternate Route

The strategies you can use to embellish armoire doors are as unlimited as your imagination. Here are just a few ideas:

▶ Create the look of raised panels by using narrow moldings to form small or large squares on the doors. Highlight the center of each panel with fabric, paint, or metallic leaf.

▶ Decoupage painted doors with photographs, prints torn from old books, or designs cut from decoupage paper or old wallpaper books.

▶ If your armoire has raised-panel doors, use a saw to remove the center panels; replace them with textured glass or colored acrylic. Install a light inside the armoire to produce a pleasing glow.

Can-Do Playroom

DESIGNED BY **HILDI**

1 BUCKETS OF IMAGINATION What can you do with a ceiling besides paint it? Why not give it architectural panache that will turn heads? A plethora of paint cans dress the "fifth wall" of this room; their circular forms repeat the circles in the wallcovering.

2 SEEING CIRCLES Wrapping paper gives these walls their graphic groove. The design is busy enough that only a discerning eye will notice that the patterns aren't perfectly matched. Glue and gift wrap are all you need to get started.

3 BOLD STROKES Kids tend to gravitate toward the brightest colors in the crayon box, so bold colors are a wise choice in a playroom. Gleaning their bright colors from the wallcovering, the playroom furnishings are ready for action. The solid colors ground the patterned walls.

4 HAVE A BALL Themed rooms can seem trite or over-the-top. In this room, simple decorative accents such as these gumballs hint at playfulness without forcing the theme.

5 MIXED SIGNALS When a room has a patterned backdrop, wall hangings may struggle for the limelight. Wide matting in a solid color can ease the tension. Here splatter-paint creations float on white paper, unfazed by the busy background.

6 ENOUGH IS ENOUGH Knowing when to stop is crucial in design. A single blue circle on this white ottoman is striking in its simplicity. Adding more circles to this low-rider could have spiraled the room into graphic overload.

Things are looking up for this formerly unfocused room. Hundreds of paint cans hang upside down from the ceiling, seemingly splashing gallons of color all over. The owners wanted a playroom, and Hildi delivered this playful, color-happy space inspired by gumballs and gift wrap.

Like a rock star who doesn't know when to quit, this room kept humming along—a bit out of tune, but humming nonetheless. Its heyday as an in-home music studio had long passed, yet the owners' guitars and framed platinum records remained. "This is our confused room, as I like to call it," one owner says.

Confused it is, with the jumble of musical mementos, a rocking horse, and various children's toys. Hildi vows to clear up the confusion and give the room a sense of purpose. She plans to transform it into a spirited playroom inspired by gumballs.

After covering the walls in wrapping paper featuring mod circles in upbeat colors, Hildi lets loose on the ceiling, installing sparkling-new empty paint cans overhead. The cans bring architectural detail to a room that had none; their rims repeat the circular motif. The inside bottoms of the cans are painted yellow, pink, blue, and other hues, so kids down below look up to see color-happy dots that mimic gumballs. "We have every color in the gumball rainbow," Hildi says.

It seems she has every unused paint can in town too. Hildi's plan calls for a whopping 650 cans to be screwed upside down and side by side into the ceiling

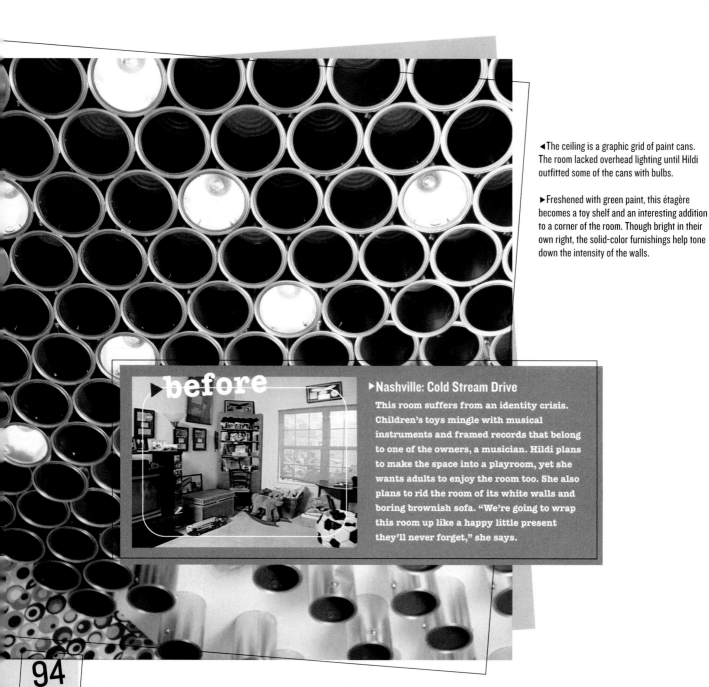

◄ The ceiling is a graphic grid of paint cans. The room lacked overhead lighting until Hildi outfitted some of the cans with bulbs.

► Freshened with green paint, this étagère becomes a toy shelf and an interesting addition to a corner of the room. Though bright in their own right, the solid-color furnishings help tone down the intensity of the walls.

► **Nashville: Cold Stream Drive**

This room suffers from an identity crisis. Children's toys mingle with musical instruments and framed records that belong to one of the owners, a musician. Hildi plans to make the space into a playroom, yet she wants adults to enjoy the room too. She also plans to rid the room of its white walls and boring brownish sofa. "We're going to wrap this room up like a happy little present they'll never forget," she says.

► **before**

▲Accessories are a quick way to give a lackluster room visual interest. Shapely accents, including a talking globe and towering alliums in a white vase, repeat this room's circular motif without calling too much attention to themselves.

for a wall-to-wall effect. Some of the cans will be outfitted with 40-watt bulbs to create downlights, a welcome touch in a room with no other overhead lighting. Amy Wynn begins taping and bolting cans together to create the core unit. However, Murphy's Law soon takes over: The process of drilling holes in the cans and ceiling and installing anchors and screws is too time-consuming for a two-day room redo. Hildi is forced to downgrade her wall-to-wall plan and adopt a more modest installation: She'll stagger the cans out from the core unit to the corners.

Hildi chalks it up to a cool idea with a difficult installation. However, the can conundrum has not burst her bubble from a design standpoint. "It's graphic," Hildi says. "It's all about the color, the spheres."

It's also loads of fun, and for a playroom, that's the main point.

◄To up the intrigue, introduce a theme in subtle ways. This round ottoman, painted with a blue circle and outfitted with round legs, quietly emphasizes the circular theme. If you don't have an existing ottoman to update, make your own. Put foam atop a board, cover the foam with batting, and then add fabric. The legs on this ottoman are actually lamppost finials. To save money, Hildi layered 1-inch-thick sheets of foam rather than using more-expensive 4-inch-thick foam.

Theme Scene

Themed rooms can work for kids and adults. Here are some tips for designing a fresh and inspired theme.

▶ **Give it a name.** Take a cue from many designers and put a label on your room design. This will jump-start your imagination and keep you focused as you shop for fabrics and accessories. The name can be specific ("Under the Big Top") or inspirational ("Romantic Retreat").

▶ **Avoid clichés.** A room decked out in anchors and lighthouses or cowboy hats and chaps can quickly become tiresome. If your design calls for stereotypical items, introduce them in unexpected ways. An oar can be turned into a curtain rod for a tab-top valance in a nautical-theme room. Walls with a painted faux-leather look hint at Western style.

▶ **Evoke a mood.** Use colors, fabrics, and textures to shape a theme. Fire-engine red energizes and stimulates—perfect for a playroom. A deep brick red makes a room seem cozy and quiet—nice for a den. Bamboo and wicker create a casual or exotic look. Shiny silk says glitz and glam.

▶ **Be subtle.** An in-your-face themed room seems staged, like a theater set. So unless you're decorating a child's room and are prepared to change it when the latest cartoon character becomes passé, be subtle. A theme that reveals itself slowly is much more intriguing and leaves room for interpretation.

▲ "It doesn't seem very Hildi." So said Paige when she helped construct this fabric-covered bulletin board. The often-seen project has a modern-minded look with a clean white backdrop and an eye-popping mix of bias tape. The tape crisscrosses to form diamonds that ensure the room isn't a sea of circles.

Down in the forest
something stirred:
It was only the note
of a bird.
Harold Simpson

▲Pine grain patterns are nature's own abstract art. Affordable plywood squares can dress up a wall. Blackboard squares provide visual relief and space for messages.

Chic Plywood and Blackboard Paneling

Conceal wall woes and add textural interest to any room. Punctuate the look with a mini blackboard for drama and practicality.

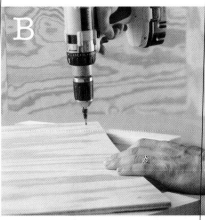

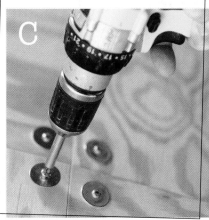

Remove the base and crown moldings from the wall. Prefinish the plywood squares with clear polyurethane or tung oil. Paint one or more hardboard squares with blackboard paint (A). Let all squares dry.

Figure out how many whole squares will fit across and up the wall. Use a circular saw to cut any squares to fit, if needed.

Predrill the corners of each square, positioning the holes 1 inch in from the sides (B).

Measure and mark the square size along each end of the wall and along the top and bottom of the wall. Connect the marks with chalk lines to create guidelines for positioning each square.

Position the squares on the wall one at a time, ensure they are level, and use a pencil to mark the wall through each corner hole. Set all squares aside. At every new pencil mark, drive toggle anchors into the wall. Position a plywood square to align with the anchors. Position a fender washer to align with one corner hole on the plywood. Secure the plywood with screws (C). Repeat the process to hang all the squares.

MATERIALS

- 2×2-foot pine plywood squares, enough to cover accent wall (available at some home centers precut, or pay to have them cut)
- Clear polyurethane or tung oil
- Precut 2×2-foot hardboard square(s) (for blackboard)
- Blackboard paint
- Plastic toggle anchors for ⅜- to ½-inch drywall or zinc drywall anchors
- 1¼-inch-diameter fender washers
- Pan-head screws, #10 1-inch

TOOLS

- Paintbrushes
- Tape measure
- Circular saw
- Drill
- Pencil
- Chalk line
- Carpenter's level
- Electric screwdriver or screwdriver bit for drill

Blackboard Paint Basics You've seen the *Trading Spaces* designers use blackboard paint a number of times to give a fun or funky spin to a room. This project proves the look can be chic too. Follow these basics to brush on a blackboard at your house:

- ▶ Sand the surface lightly with fine-grit sandpaper and wipe away residue with a tack cloth.
- ▶ Prime the surface; let dry.
- ▶ Brush, roll, or spray on the blackboard paint; let dry according to the package directions.
- ▶ Plan on painting a second coat and possibly a third coat; follow the manufacturer's recommendations for drying times between coats. Let the paint dry before writing on the surface.

In the hands of the *Trading Spaces* designers, boxy rooms and ho-hum furniture gain "wow" power with a few easy additions such as these.

Building Character

Molding Basics

Walls, ceilings, and door and drawer fronts all can be transformed into new creations when you dress them up—lavishly or simply—with moldings.

Home centers now stock a tremendous variety of moldings. In fact, all the moldings *right* came from only one aisle in one store. You'll find moldings in lengths from 6 to 16 feet, and most are made of softwood—usually pine. Some of the more popular moldings, such as crown molding, come in hardwood too—most often oak.

To butt-join moldings, as shown *opposite bottom,* use a circular or handsaw and cut the pieces so their ends are square. If you want to create mitered corners use a miter box and backsaw as shown *below.* Whenever possible, hold a piece of molding in place where you plan to install it and then mark the cut line for a more accurate fit.

Place the piece of molding in the miter box and sight down the blade of the saw. Align the saw with the mark. Hold the molding against the back of the miter box, grasping the wood tightly so it will not slide as you cut it.

To install moldings without cutting miter joints, use plinth blocks (also called rosettes), *opposite center,* at the corners and joints. The square-cut ends of the moldings abut the sides of the blocks.

To install moldings, you'll need everything shown in the photograph *opposite:* a measuring tape for determining accurate dimensions, a carpenter's level to ensure that the moldings are perfectly horizontal or vertical, a hammer and finishing nails to secure the moldings to the surface, and a nail puller to

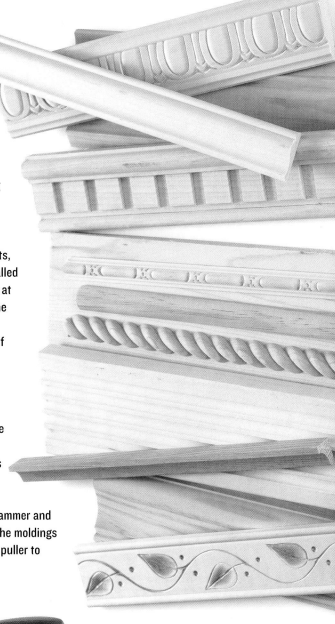

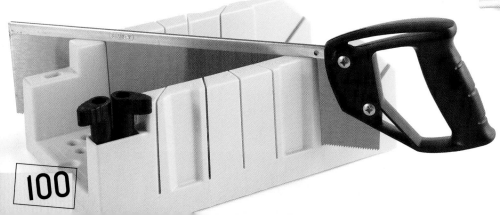

remove bent nails. Use a nail set to drive the heads of the finishing nails below the wood surface. Fill the holes with wood filler; after it dries, use a sanding block to smooth it. Wipe away the residue with a tack cloth.

Plinth blocks

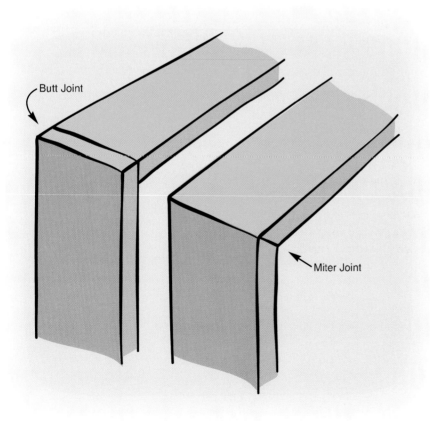

Butt Joint

Miter Joint

Tips for Success

▶ To save time, paint or stain moldings before installation. Then touch up nail holes once the lengths are in place and the wood filler is dry.

▶ If you will be driving a nail within 3 inches of the edge of a piece, drill a pilot hole to prevent thin moldings from splitting.

▶ Attach short pieces of molding to a surface by using construction adhesive.

▶ Drive in only as many nails as you need to hold the piece firmly against the wall or the door or drawer front.

Moldings are only one option for adding architectural interest to a room or a piece of furniture. Consider these alternatives:

Another Route

Keep Your Eyes Peeled

Look beyond the molding aisle for other architectural features and materials that can enhance your room designs.

MDF (medium-density fiberboard) can be cut to various sizes and shapes and used to add dimensional effects similar to moldings—often at lower cost. MDF must be painted.

Brackets come in ornate and clean-lined varieties. They can play a supporting role for open shelves or make a cameo appearance as decorative assets in the upper corners of passageways.

Embossed wallpapers—full-width rolls or borders—can be used on walls, doors, and drawers. Cover an entire wall or create wainscoting. Some embossed papers can be painted to mimic leather, tin, and other materials.

Onlays can be purchased from woodworking stores and home centers. These small, ornate wood pieces lend character to plain pieces of furniture and cabinetry. Secure onlays to the wood surface with glue and/or brads.

Architectural salvage, such as this tin medallion and the plinth molding beside it, can be found at salvage yards, flea markets, garage sales, and auctions. Use salvaged pieces to adorn furniture, walls, or even the exposed sides of staircases.

Tile can be more than a floor covering or backsplash. Purchase a select few to punctuate a wall. Line up the tiles in a row—like a staccato chair rail—or install them randomly to achieve the look you want.

Rope is an affordable, textural alternative to molding. Use a hot-glue gun and lengths of rope to create a bead at the ceiling or around doors and windows. Or create a paneled look on walls, using rope instead of wood.

Architectural
Tricks

Every space seems more interesting when you introduce new dimension. These *Trading Spaces* rooms offer up ideas that could bring depth and style to your abode too.

1 DESIGNED BY DOUG

2 DESIGNED BY KIA

1 SPOTLIGHT CABINETRY It's difficult to imagine that these kitchen cabinets in Miramar: Avenue 164 used to have plain white slab doors and drawers. Doug specifies the addition of lath strips, which give the surfaces a paneled look, and then jazzes things up with sunny Caribbean colors.

2 SALVAGE STYLE Architectural pieces rescued from old buildings and homes are precious elements for creating new style. In Virginia: Gentle Heights Court, Kia brings in these blue-stained ancient-looking columns to enhance a Far Eastern theme in the bedroom. The shelves on the wall beyond are fashioned from a salvaged storage pallet.

3 FINESSE A FIREPLACE Does your fireplace look exactly like the one in your neighbor's home? Study Gen's work in Austin: Wampton Way. The custom-built facade she designs features fluted wood panels elegantly painted in black and punctuated with a stained wood mantel.

4 STACK UP PERSONALITY Say goodbye to a boxy room when you dress it up in layers of moldings. In North Carolina: Dogwood Trail, Vern uses three colors to multiply the dimensional effect of the moldings: Brown boards topped with narrow dark green boards create a stylish grid pattern against pale green walls.

5 MOLD SOME ROMANCE Fluted moldings and plinth blocks wear a regal coat of ivory paint and form a budget-conscious headboard in San Diego: Duenda Road. Frank romances the new architecture with yards of sheer ivory chiffon, gracefully swagged from ceiling to floor.

4 DESIGNED BY VERN

3 DESIGNED BY GENEVIEVE

5 DESIGNED BY FRANK

105

Chapter Four

Art

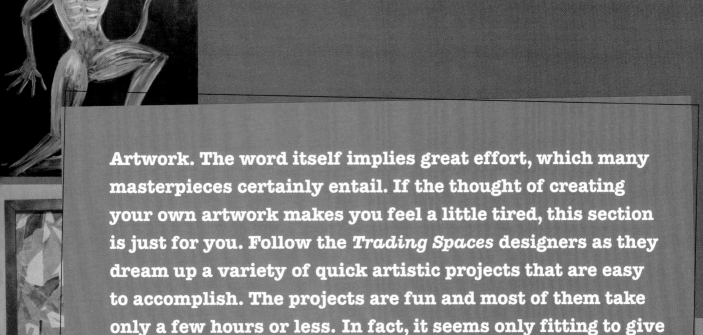

Artwork. The word itself implies great effort, which many masterpieces certainly entail. If the thought of creating your own artwork makes you feel a little tired, this section is just for you. Follow the *Trading Spaces* designers as they dream up a variety of quick artistic projects that are easy to accomplish. The projects are fun and most of them take only a few hours or less. In fact, it seems only fitting to give these creations a new label: art *easy!*

work
Made Easy

Mediterranean Modern

4

With a wayward furniture arrangement, this living room needed help. Laurie's commonsense approach creates a better flow and puts collectibles and artwork front and center.

DESIGNED BY **LAURIE**

1 COLLECTED CHARACTER Whatever possessions obsess you—vintage purses, plates, or baseball caps—they'll gain impact when grouped together. This is especially true of small accessories. Here upholstered panels anchor and unify a collection of crosses.

2 BLANK SLATE White walls give this room a modern gallery look that allows the artwork to shine. Cushy upholstered pieces kick in coziness.

3 BEAM ME UP Though not as substantial as real beams, these strips of wood nailed to the ceiling are an artful addition to an often overlooked surface. Using wood strips instead of real beams is a budget-friendly timesaver.

4 SHELF TRICK Although these shelves seem to float on the wall, they're actually adhered to a white board that blends into the wall. The clever design streamlines the setting and adds contemporary flair.

5 POP ART The blues and golds that color the room play up the hues in this Warholian painting. Facing hundreds of paint chips can be overwhelming. To make the choice easier, take your inspiration piece—artwork or fabric—to the paint store and order a custom blend to match it.

6 FOOTLOOSE If you're short on space, let an ottoman serve as a footrest and a coffee table. This ottoman sports a casual new slipcover; batting placed over the top of the ottoman adds a fluffy layer.

▼Travertine tiles dry-laid into this coffee table offer a hardworking surface with Mediterranean flair.

before

▶Austin: Govalle Avenue

This living room has a quasi-Cubist quality. The furniture arrangement is oddly fragmented, creating an awkward flow throughout the room. The wall hangings are nondescript, and the owners' collection of crosses is ineffectively displayed. Laurie plans to unify the room by repositioning the furniture. She'll also create focal points with new (and newly arranged) artwork.

The owners of this home had grounded their living room in sentimental stuff, most notably a collection of metal crosses and a Warholian painting of their children that was done by a relative. Sadly, their prized possessions had little impact in the space, which was chockablock with furniture positioned in a puzzling arrangement. "I would love for it to either all come together or just create two separate spaces," one owner says.

Using the painting as her inspiration, Laurie takes a leap with a modernized Mediterranean design. The transformation starts with white paint. The words "cozy" and "white" rarely appear together; here, however, the white warms up near the earth tones of the furniture. "It is the perfect background for this warm furniture to contrast against," Laurie says.

The white background creates a gallerylike feel, making the wall hangings seem more important.

▲ This painting of the homeowners' children was done by a relative. Experiment with your own family photos to create something similar. Take photos to a copy store and have them converted to different colors or use specialty photo-imaging software on your home computer to manipulate scanned images. Mount your creations on a painted canvas or hardboard.

◄ Items from a collection gain importance when grouped together. Though the owner had hung her crosses together, they were too small individually to make much of an impact. Laurie covered two boards with batting and a natural-weave fabric and then attached three crosses to each panel to give the collection more prominence. "All of them pop off this neutral background," she says.

►After relocating the TV armoire to the wall opposite the sofa, Laurie placed the upholstered pieces in a more sensible—and multifunctional—arrangement. Matching upholstered chairs face off from opposite ends of the long room. This setup unifies the space, while two area rugs define more-intimate furniture groupings within the larger scheme.

► This chair and new coffee table have a similar boxy shape; coating both in chocolate brown paint unifies them even more. If you've collected a mix of furnishings over the years, paint them the same color and watch a new look come together.

▲ Accent pillows fashioned from eyelash fabric and a striped print introduce pattern into the room. Their white backgrounds contrast with the upholstered furniture.

Above the sofa, a large mirror flanked by shelves breaks up an expanse of wall and defines the main sitting area. Six crosses, carefully selected from a much larger collection, are showcased on two upholstered boards that anchor a sitting area at the far end of the room. Thanks to Laurie's presentation skills, the cross collection is now substantial enough to command attention even from the front entrance. The Warhol-inspired painting energizes an adjacent wall. Its blue background connects with the fabrics throughout the room.

Tapping into the artistic abilities of her team, Laurie also gives the homeowners a new piece of contemporary artwork. The 5-foot-square canvas creation features an orange pinwheel-like design. The piece balances the bulky armoire and brings a jolt of color to one wall.

Laurie takes the drama up a level by adding faux ceiling beams. "It was so simple," Laurie says of the project, which required little more than a hammer and nails. Down below, two area rugs add cushy comfort and define the furniture groupings—one area for watching TV and one area for quiet conversation or relaxing. The light hues of the rugs contrast with the chocolate brown coffee table and other furnishings.

With total expenditures at $985.63, Laurie leaves about $15 on the table. The room is comfortably filled to the brim, and Laurie was able to reuse much of the existing artwork, accessories, and furniture. Though not new, the rearranged pieces give the room a refreshing new attitude.

"I would never have thought to arrange it in this fashion—ever," one owner says.

► A white-painted board suspends two brown shelves: The contrast in color gives the illusion of free-floating shelves. "That's part of the Mediterranean modern," Laurie says.

◄Laurie lucked out with her team: Both of them have artistic ability. Taking advantage of their skills, Laurie commissioned them to create a masterpiece in one night. They came up with this striking modern pinwheel-like design. "That's fabulous," Laurie says, noting that the swirl of color has the "vitality of a sunflower," with south-of-France, Mediterranean influence.

Great Groupings

The old adage "There's strength in numbers" applies to artwork. Grouping pictures, prints, or collectibles can turn a plain wall into a focal point. These tips will help you arrange your art for maximum impact. For more tips on art arrangements, turn to page 135.

▶ **Consider the space.** Generally, walls with more width than height call for horizontal groupings; narrow spaces welcome vertical arrangements. Arrange shapes within an imaginary framework with a strong horizontal element. Keep spaces between frames equal. To create intimacy, hang pictures low so they visually link with furniture.

▶ **Frame for personality.** Frames and mats are meant to complement your artwork, not compete with it. Modern art often looks best in minimal frames made of metal; traditional paintings call for carved wood frames and multilayered mats. Let the image, not your room palette, guide mat color. Mats in dark hues are dramatic; white mats emphasize the art itself. Mats twice as wide as the frame are standard and give the eye a resting point; tiny pictures with oversize mats are eye-catching.

▶ **Get the picture.** To avoid making Swiss cheese out of your walls, arrange pictures on the floor on a large piece of paper (or taped-together pieces of kraft paper), trace around the frames, and then tape the paper to the wall as a map for nail holes. Or cut paper templates of each picture, tape them to the wall, and move them around until you like the look.

Easy Painted Canvases

Introduce blockbuster style into any room with these three-dimensional blocks of color.

Select pairs of paint colors that contrast and/or complement each other. Paint the walls and woodwork white; let dry.

Mark off the desired number of blocks on each wall, positioning each block 12 inches from the sides, top, and bottom of each wall. Use a long carpenter's level to check that lines are straight. Outline the markings with painter's tape (A).

Apply the desired paint color inside the taped area (B). (For smooth results, roll on paint in a W and then roll across those strokes to fill in the block.) Let dry; apply a second coat of color, if needed. Remove the tape (C).

Paint canvases in contrasting colors. For a quick, even finish, use the paint roller.

Install picture-hanging hardware on the back of each canvas. Use a hammer and finishing nails to hang the canvases on the walls within the color-block areas as desired (D).

► **MATERIALS**

Interior latex paint (white, plus 2 colors per wall)

Artist's canvases (24×24 inches and 30×40 inches are shown)

Picture-hanging hardware

Finishing nails

► **TOOLS**

Paintbrushes, paint rollers and tray

Tape measure

Pencil

Carpenter's level

Low-tack painter's tape

Hammer

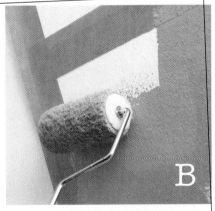
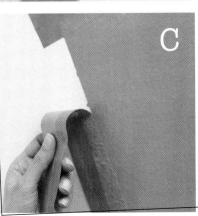
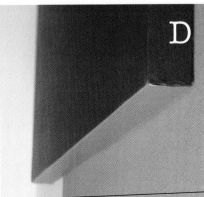

The Alternate Route **Personalize this project with these variations:**

► Rather than cover the entire canvas with one solid color, tape off one or more broad stripes. Alternate colors, if desired.

► Use tape to create diagonal swaths of color on the walls or on the canvases.

► Stencil or stamp shapes or designs onto the canvases. (See pages 170–171 for more information.)

► Have a copy store photocopy favorite snapshots onto canvas squares and cut to the desired size. Leave broad white canvas borders around the images to serve as mats. Stretch canvases onto frames fashioned from 2×2s, staple the canvases to the frames, and hang them on walls painted with color blocks.

◄ What could be more ideal than starting your day in a room wrapped in all the colors you love? Painted canvases offer the perfect opportunity to bring in an entire palette of happy hues or just a few colors—you get to choose.

Red-Hot Romance

A lifeless bedroom becomes a happening honeymoon suite as Rick turns up the heat with robust artwork and a design that's sure to keep the sparks flying.

1

3

4

2

DESIGNED BY **RICK**

1 HEADS UP This towering plywood headboard doubles as modern art. A mixture resembling copper paste gives the smaller squares and rectangles luster and texture that mimics the look of metal.

2 PASSIONATE PAIRING Although red is the color of romance, it's also part of the primary palette and can have kid-room connotations. Paired with black, though, red quickly grows up. Black intensifies the lushness of this shimmering red duvet cover, taking the room to the sensuous side. The color combination is bold enough to balance the dramatic headboard.

3 GEOMETRY LESSON If you want a room to say mod, hip, or cool, give it a graphic punch. Repeat common geometric shapes such as circles or squares for impact. This smattering of rectangular pillows in copper, red, and black echoes the geometric grid on the headboard.

4 SWOOPING IN Everyday furnishings sometimes function as art. The sensuous curves of these lamps engage the eye and soften the angles of the nightstand and headboard.

5 MIRROR IMAGE Melding style with function, the geometric design used for the headboard repeats as a frame for this mirror.

6 ILLUSIONS OF GRANDEUR Designers love to play tricks with windows. A wall—not windows—lurks behind this cascading red panel. Extending the window treatment makes the window seem wider, the space grander. The red fabric teams with a copper-color sheer panel that softly diffuses light.

7 OPPOSITES ATTRACT Contrast gives a room rhythm. This room goes all out in playing light colors against dark—copper-metal color against dark wood, and chrome against a copper-hued backdrop.

◄Simple as it may look, this canvas painting actually took three people to complete. Making a game out of the process, Rick gave Paige and his two team members each 10 minutes to work his or her magic on the black canvas, with the next person picking up where the other left off. The last team member to wield the brush painted over her husband's and Paige's rather busy contributions, obliterating their work with a coat of black. Then she added a single white squiggle. "When I see what it is now, I really hate what I did," Paige says.

Excuses, excuses. The newlywed owners of this home had two good ones when explaining away their beige-box bedroom: Planning their wedding had eaten up all of their free time, and they've only been in their house a few months. Rick is ready to give them a belated wedding present by wrapping their room in romance.

Romance, though, comes in many forms. There's the soft, simmering-slowly kind. And then there's the red-hot, sparks-are-a-flying kind that Rick chooses.

Rick's sizzling color scheme of red, black, and copper gives the room a sexy, sultry vibe—a bit masculine, a bit boudoirish. This is one of the few *Trading Spaces* rooms where the boldest color doesn't come from a paint can. Rick reserves the red for the fabrics and gives the walls a relatively conservative coat that complements the copper. "It's a good base without being uncommitted," Rick says.

Next, Rick and Amy Wynn create the main focal point in this bedroom: Two 4×8-foot oak plywood

▲Some furnishings—this armoire included—have an aversion to paint or stain. To darken the light armoire, Rick applied a special gel-form stain designed for wood, fiberglass, metal, and other surfaces. "Their furniture is some sort of an 'other surface,'" Rick explains. The armoire now sports a two-tone treatment that echoes the look of the headboard.

before

▶**Nashville: Murphywood Crossing**
This bedroom is far from finished. In fact, it hasn't even been started. There's no headboard. The light furnishings blend into the white walls. White blinds at the windows are stark, with no fabric to soften the harshness. Rick's plan calls for bold-color fabrics and accessories, lots of paint and stain, and dramatic sculptural pieces that also have a functional role.

▶Building furniture to fit the space provides a good opportunity to increase function. The nightstand tabletop, custom-built by Amy Wynn, features a workhorse below: A wicker basket slips inside the lower box to add texture and hide clutter.

strips, enhanced with dark walnut stain, march parallel up a wall to form the foundation for a dramatic 3-D headboard. Smaller squares and rectangles cut from MDF are coated with Rick's special potion—a mixture that includes bronzing powder and joint compound—and take on the look of textured metal; these are attached to the oak panels in a random pattern. The result is a contemporary appliqué piece, with a striking juxtaposition of light against dark and grainy wood against shiny faux metal.

And so it goes throughout the room. The contrasting elements used for the headboard repeat in smaller scale to become a stylish mirror frame. A similar dark-against-light scheme refreshes the armoire and dresser. You'll also see chrome thrown into the mix: Silvery

◀Metals bring a rich quality to any room. Chrome lamps contrast with the copper-tone squares on the mirror frame and the brassy pulls on the dresser. Flickering candles soften the setting.

lamps on the dresser and nightstands mingle with the coppery elements on the headboard and mirror and the copper-tone fabric on the pillows.

The final tally for this modern-day love story was $999.53—not even enough left to throw in a red rose.

Balancing Act

Whether you're thinking of splurging on a piece of art or a king-size bed, factor in these elements to help bring harmony to your room:

▶ **Size.** Varying the sizes, including heights, of furnishings and accessories will visually stimulate a room. Think big: Most people make the mistake of going too small with furnishings and accessories. (Picture the common sight of a too-small painting above a large sofa.) Even a small space usually can benefit from a large item; one good-size piece can make the room seem grander.

▶ **Proportion.** The relationship of one furniture piece to another is also important to good design. Build your design around the largest furnishing in the room, then add other furnishings, using a critical eye to judge how well they fit within the scheme.

▶ **Color.** Some colors carry more visual weight than others and can quickly throw a room off balance if used with a heavy hand. A little bit of red, for example, weighs in big. Black is another heavyweight. It's a great grounding element and worth adding in to every scheme, even if it's only in a picture frame or matting around a print.

▶ **Repetition.** Far from being overkill, repetition can create cohesiveness in a room. Toss the same color around a room—in a pillow, a painting, or a frame, for example—to keep the eye moving and to unify the space. Repetition need not be literal. An oversize vertical mirror can mimic the look of a floor-to-ceiling window.

◀The baseball is a nod to the man of the house; the bench is a hit with both owners. Spanning nearly the full width of the window and topped with a red cushion, the bench—which Amy Wynn created by layering platforms atop one another—has the look of a cozy built-in window seat. Its boxy shape repeats the design used throughout the room.

▲Nesting tables offer clean lines and flat surfaces that are ideal for decoupage projects. These tables are dressed up with precut wallpaper shapes, which come in colorful squares, stripes, flowers, and other attractive designs.

Decoupage Nesting Tables

Paper cutouts and paint transform plain nesting tables into colorful artistic accents.

A

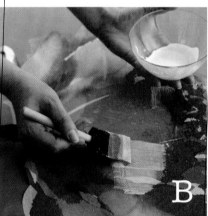

B

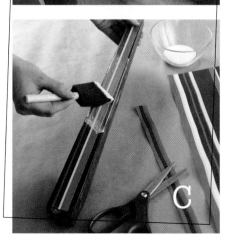

C

Prior to assembly, lightly sand the tables with fine-grit sandpaper. Wipe the surfaces clean with a tack cloth. Brush on primer; let dry. Paint on base coat color; let dry.

Use sharp scissors to cut out the decoupage designs. (See "Decoupage Possibilities" *below right* for cutting tips.)

Using a paintbrush or foam brush, apply decoupage medium to the back of each cutout (A) and adhere to the tabletop and legs as desired. If excess decoupage medium seeps from beneath the cutouts, wipe it away with a damp sponge. If needed, use a wallpaper brush to flatten the edges of the papers so they adhere to the project surface. Smooth out any air bubbles.

After all motifs are in position, use a foam brush to apply decoupage medium in two or three thin, even layers to all the decorated surfaces (B and C); allow the medium to dry between coats. Seal all decorated surfaces with one or more coats of clear poly-acrylic.

Assemble the tables as instructed by the manufacturer.

▶ **MATERIALS**
Nesting tables, ready to assemble
Primer
Latex or acrylic crafts paint, in desired colors
Decoupage designs
Decoupage medium
Clear poly-acrylic

▶ **TOOLS**
Sandpaper, fine-grit
Tack cloth
Paintbrushes
Scissors
Disposable foam brushes
Sponge
Wallpaper brush

Decoupage Possibilities Special decoupage papers, like these *Trading Spaces* border cutouts and murals, are available at crafts and art supply stores as well as on the Internet. Wallpaper, wrapping paper, greeting cards, scrapbooking paper, reproduction prints, or other heavier papers can also be used for decoupage projects. Avoid magazine and newspaper cutouts; the thin paper allows the reverse side of the image to bleed through when you apply the decoupage medium. Use a small pair of very sharp scissors to cut out the motifs. Hold the scissors at an angle close to the edge of the motif as you cut; turn the paper as you cut so that you get a clean edge. Alternatively, use a crafts knife and a self-healing cutting mat.

Classically
Inclined

1

If walls could talk, this living room would say a big thank-you to Edward. He turned a blank-slate room into a warm and inviting European enclave by adding rich color and using artwork in unexpected ways.

1 ARTFUL ENDEAVOR A canvas painting found at a thrift store steps into a new role as a smart and stylish covering for the doors of a classically styled computer station. The Italian-inspired artwork breaks up what would otherwise be a big, boring expanse of brown against olive walls. It also provides eye-level visual interest for seated residents and guests.

2 LOOKING UP Painting the ceiling yellow casts a glow on the room. The white crown molding—artwork in its own right—bridges the olive wall and golden ceiling.

3 STAGE SETTER Olive walls give the room an intimate quality and provide a rich backdrop for artwork. The saturated color also visually fills in gaps where there is no artwork.

4 SCULPTURAL ADDITION Instead of a predictable floral arrangement, a bountiful urn raises the visual plane of this seating area. It goes beyond bouquet, acting more as a piece of three-dimensional sculpture.

5 SINK IN With their clean lines and formfitting slipcovers, two slipper chairs backed with bolster pillows bring contemporary flair to the traditional room. The low profile of the chairs makes it possible to position them near the opening to the dining room without obstructing the line of sight.

6 COLOR CONNECTION Fabric panels soften a wall and ease the transition between the olive living room and red dining room. The striped fabric incorporates all the colors used in the two rooms.

DESIGNED BY **EDWARD**

127

before

▶Pennsylvania: Hillcrest Drive

This living room has a case of the blahs. Nearly everything is beige, and the space feels empty. Wall hangings consist of two framed photographs and a wreath; the wall above the sofa is a blank slate. To make the space more intimate and conducive to conversation, Edward wants to add color and reposition the furniture. He also plans to create a more stylish home for the computer equipment, in a large armoire (beige, of course). In addition to giving the room personality, Edward intends to design the space so it will harmonize with the adjoining dining room.

◄Repositioning furniture, including moving it away from walls, can dramatically alter the look of a room—without costing a penny. A pair of velvet slipper chairs faces off with the sofa to create a functional conversation area in this living room. By placing the sofa against the window, which is dressed with a velvet valance and billowy panels, Edward created a focal point and solved the problem of what to hang above the sofa.

Too bare, too beige, too bland. It didn't take a trained eye to sum up the woes of this living room. And it didn't seem like a tall order when one of the owners said he'd like a design with a "bit of shock value" to it. After being used to all things beige—walls, carpet, draperies, and furniture—adding color will be the first thing to make it more exciting.

Edward knows this room can only improve; however, he still faces a challenge: The owners recently swathed the adjacent dining room with red damask wallpaper, and because the living room has an open view of the space, continuity will be essential.

Edward approaches the blank-canvas room like an artist about to begin a masterpiece.

Though the look he creates is classical and traditional, with a distinct European influence, it also delivers visual excitement. The olive green paint he chooses for the walls initially elicits less-than-favorable comments. "This is the closest to baby poop I've seen on *Trading Spaces*," Paige says when she first steps into the room. Name-calling aside, the color darkens as it dries and soon wins the approval of the team.

The newly dubbed Tuscan Olive walls create a lush, rich backdrop for artwork—something the room sorely lacks. Knowing he will buy no Picassos on a *Trading Spaces* budget, Edward tears botanical prints from an old calendar, one of his favorite art-for-nothing quick fixes. Framed and grouped en masse, the prints turn one wall into a colorful garden. A 1970s painting picked up at a thrift store for $25

▲Rather than discard a perfectly good piece of furniture, Edward dyed the owners' existing sofa to tone down its whiteness and then gussied it up with nailhead trim and flirty fringe.

◄Detailed with grapes and a flowing vine, the owners' existing metal end table and coffee table were perfectly suited to Edward's vision for the room. Urns add a classic touch to a room, as does tapestry fabric, which Edward used to make pillows.

finds a new home as a stylish facade on the doors of the computer armoire. "I thought, 'Well, it could be a picture picture, but why just do something traditional?'" Edward says.

The team members are still slightly worried about the olive green paint, especially in relation to the red wallpaper in the adjoining dining room. Their worries are put to rest, however, when Edward shows them the drapery fabric, which brings together all the colors in the two rooms.

In the end, the owners get the shock value they desired, in a good way. As one owner puts it, "This is more than I could have ever imagined."

▲Fabric is a great starting point for any room. Edward devotes about one-third of his budget to fabric, and it is money well-spent. The striped fabric used for these draperies pulls together the red in the adjoining dining room, the olive on the living room walls, and the golden tone on the living room ceiling.

◄A pair of ottomans dressed in coffee-color slipcovers with brown velvet piping is ready for action yet is stylish when not in use. Think beyond seating pieces when considering slipcovers. For example, use them to dress up utilitarian items such as storage containers or toy boxes.

▼Edward created an impressive display with 12 framed botanical prints. The frames hang in a precise grid; the prints themselves, torn from old calendar pages, have irregular edges. To help control how the edges tear for your own artwork, dip a foam brush in water, wet the perimeters of the paper at the desired finished size, and gently tear. Use spray adhesive to mount each print. Here, black paper serves as a mat and offers eye-popping contrast. For more easy artwork ideas, see "Walls That Wow" *right* and page 134.

Walls That Wow:
Art on a Budget

No matter how great the furniture or how perfect the window treatments, a room with blank walls will always feel incomplete. If you'd rather not drop hundreds or thousands of dollars on a single piece of wall art, consider these options:

▶ **Warm up the walls with color.** White walls, which have the look of a gallery, almost demand showy artwork. If you're short on wall hangings, paint walls a rich color, such as deep green or eggplant; the color will help fill in the gaps.

▶ **Hang a grouping** of inexpensive prints instead of one large, expensive piece of artwork. Related items, such as a series of gardening scenes from a calendar or old family photos, will have greater impact when grouped together.

▶ **Fool the eye.** Butt framed prints against one another to create the illusion of grandeur. Or opt for an inexpensive art poster with a do-it-yourself metal frame (skip the matting). Posters used to promote local art shows or fund-raising activities often can be purchased for a dollar or so after the event.

▶ **Forgo frames.** You'll save some money and create a clean look. Have clear acrylic cut to the desired size and use brads or glass clips to hold the acrylic-covered artwork to the wall. This works especially well for a grid of pictures that might otherwise overpower a room. This option is best reserved for casual or modern settings.

▶ **Use alternative art.** Art comes in many forms. Children's art projects, plates, tapestries, rugs, quilts, and vintage purses or hats are all worthy candidates for the wall. Old frames sitting in the attic or rescued from a flea market can be hung on the wall as is, without pictures.

Vintage Display

If your passion is collecting small vintage objects, round up some favorites and frame them for display—right on the wall.

Choose the wall where you want to display a composition of treasures. Outline the display area with moldings—cut to length, painted or stained, and mitered on the ends to form a frame. (For tips on cutting moldings, see page 100.)

Secure the moldings to the wall with finishing nails. Sink the nails below the surface of the wood with a nail set and fill the holes with wood filler. Let filler dry and lightly sand. Touch up the sanded areas with matching paint or stain.

Cut lengths of brown kraft paper and tape them together to match the size and shape of the framed area. Lay the paper on a work surface. Arrange items on top of the paper to determine an effective layout. On the paper mark positions for nails and screws.

Tape the paper to the wall inside the frame, with the marks facing out. Hang the vintage items, driving nails or screws directly through the paper; then tear the paper away from the wall. If you prefer, press the tip of a pen or pencil through the paper where the markings are, thereby transferring the marks to the wall. Remove the paper and then hang the vintage items (A).

Add brackets (B) and a shelf, if needed, to display items that can't be secured directly to the wall.

▶ MATERIALS
Moldings
Paint or stain
  (to finish the moldings)
Finishing nails
Wood filler
Sandpaper
Brown kraft paper
Low-tack painter's tape
Vintage hangers and hooks
Screws

▶ TOOLS
Miter box and backsaw
Paintbrush
Hammer
Nail set
Scissors
Pencil or pen
Electric screwdriver

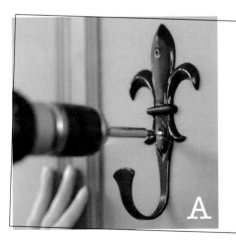

◀ Talk about being hooked! This terrific collection of iron hooks features a fascinating variety of shapes and designs to keep the eye moving. The molding frame attaches directly to the wall.

The Alternate Route.... Vintage hooks could get you thinking about all kinds of items that might work in a composition:

▶ Doorknobs
▶ Keys
▶ Plates
▶ Silverware
▶ Printing blocks and tintypes
▶ Pocket watches and alarm clocks
▶ Beaded purses
▶ Brass and iron letters and numbers

If you love it, call it art!

Art with Heart

Search the House

On *Trading Spaces* artwork is often found hiding in drawers and boxes around the house. Pretend you're Doug (or the designer of your choice) and look around your own home for potential wall art.

◀ **Vacation mementos.** Admit it—you gathered up seashells on your last trip to the ocean and left them in a basket on the back of the toilet tank for months. It's time to put them to another use. Purchase a shadow box at the crafts store and line the back with colored paper. (The backing in this shadow box is actually a page torn from a magazine; you could also use wrapping paper or an enlarged vacation photo of the ocean.) Arrange the seashells, or other objects, on the backing until you like how they look; then secure them in place with a hot-glue gun.

◀ **Other treasures.** Watch for other affordable (or free!) items to hang on the wall. Children's art, flea market or starving artist artwork, and calendar prints become wallworthy with the addition of inexpensive frames.

▲ **Family photos.** Do you have shoeboxes full of old family photos stashed in closets and in the attic? Dig out some memories and take your favorites to a copy shop to have them enlarged. A plain black metal frame and white mat make this photo of Dad with his army buddies even more special.

134

Arranging Made Easy

It's easy to imagine what your photographs, artwork, or other objects will look like on the wall when you use this "test template" strategy:

1) Lay the artwork on paper; trace. Cut out the shapes.
2) Adhere the paper templates to the wall, using low-tack painter's tape. Experiment with the grouping until you achieve an arrangement you like.
3) Nail directly through the paper (so you won't forget how you had the pieces arranged). Remove the paper and hang each piece on its nail.

▲ **Random thoughts.** If you lean toward eclecticism or have a casual room, matching frames and even rows aren't necessary. Trust your instincts and create a flowing arrangement that encourages the eye to move.

▲ **Serene symmetry.** Same-size frames and artwork grouped in a neat square become a large-scale focal point.

▶ **Think alike.** Artwork that is disparate or alike can hang together when you select matching frames and mats. This series adds drama above a sofa and would also work well above a long console table or a low storage cabinet.

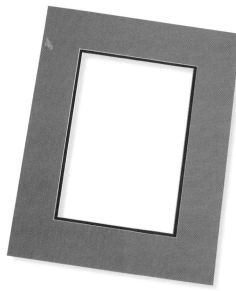

◀ To give your artwork even more interest and dimension, frame it with a double mat like this one. Select mat board in two colors that complement the artwork. Make the opening in the bottom mat ⅛ to ¼ inch smaller than the opening in the top mat.

Make Your Own Mat

Mat board and mat cutters come in a variety of sizes and prices, and both are available at art supply and crafts stores. If you plan to frame a lot of art—say, enough for your own house and some for friends—consider purchasing a mat cutter and making your own mats. Here's how:

1) Measure and mark the mat board with a T square, remove the mat guide from the mat-cutting board, and position the mat board—color side down—beneath the guide rail. Align the back of the board against the squaring bar and the cutting mark with the edge of the guide rail (A).

2) Use the straight-cutting head to cut the outside dimensions of the mat along the marks (B).

3) Switch to the bevel-cutting head and slip the mat guide back into place. Set the mat guide to create the desired border width (C). Slip a scrap piece of mat board (shown here in a rust color) beneath the guide rail so it rests on the cutting board. Choose scrap board that is at least as long as the mat you are cutting so it will protect the blade as you cut. With the edge of the mat board against the mat guide and the back of the mat board against the squaring bar, mark the inside cutting length down the full length of the board. Turn the board and make the second inside cutting mark. Repeat to finish, marking the remaining two sides.

4) Position the bevel-cutting head so that the start-and-stop indicator line aligns with the mark where you will begin cutting. Press the anticrawl pin to prevent the bevel-cutting head from creeping forward (D).

5) Push the blade holder down so the blade punctures the mat board and pull the cutting head toward you, maintaining even, downward pressure (E). Continue the cut until the start-and-stop indicator line aligns with the stopping point. (If your mat cutter features a production stop, set it to stop the blade at the desired point.) Lift the blade holder and turn the board. Repeat the steps to make the remaining three inside cuts.

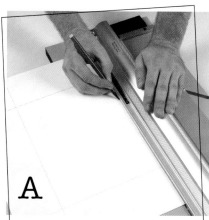

A

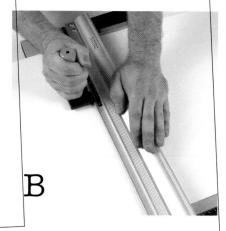

B

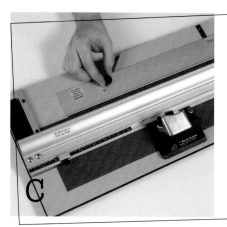

C

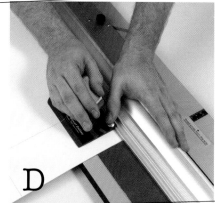

D

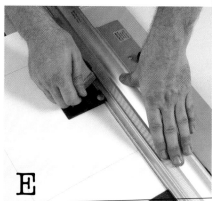

E

Mix and Match

Crafts stores are a great source for low-cost frames and mats *above*. Let the artwork and your room influence your choices when you shop. Choose mats that complement the colors in the artwork; pick frames that enhance the artwork without competing for attention.

The red frame *right* cheerfully complements the child's drawing and builds on the sense of playfulness.

Find Your Artistic Side

1 DESIGNED BY VERN

**Picture yourself painting a masterpiece ...
No? Maybe your creative genius belongs in
a different medium. These *Trading Spaces*
favorites may stir up your own artistic ideas.**

2 DESIGNED BY HILDI

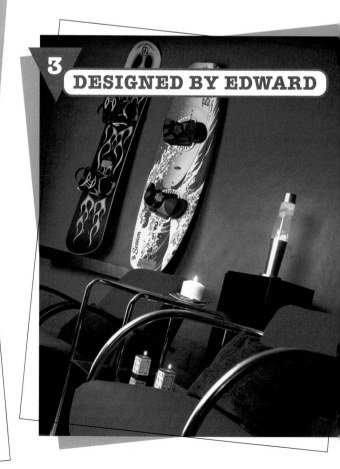

3 DESIGNED BY EDWARD

1 LET IT SHINE Glistening rows of individual crystals stand in for a traditional painting above the bedroom fireplace in Washington, D.C.: Quebec Place. Vern's deep red paint provides a backdrop that sets off the crystals. Narrow metal rods hanging from wire give the arrangement a sculptural feel. Clear glass goblet votives line up below the sparkling artwork to introduce the glow of candlelight.

2 GO FOR THE RECORD Multiples of almost any object are sure to make a visual impact in a room. Hildi reveals the artistic worth of old vinyl albums when she secures them to the wall in Texas: Ghostbridge. Record labels of various colors punctuate the graphic grid of black discs. Paint colors borrowed from the labels repeat throughout the room.

3 EVERYDAY ART Common objects can take the spotlight and serve as artwork around the house. In Tucson: Euclid Avenue, Edward builds on colors found in a pair of snowboards, slathering this apartment in supersaturated hues. Leaning the snowboards on a ledge puts them onstage as prominent works of art.

4 BOXED BEAUTY Shadow boxes can show off three-dimensional objects you love. In Pennsylvania: Hillcrest Drive, Frank establishes a relaxing seaside theme for a bedroom by filling three acrylic-face shadow boxes with calming compositions of sand, shells, and dried branches.

5 BUY A DOOR PRIZE Christi recognizes opportunity knocking when she finds a salvaged door in Pennsylvania: Stump Drive. Using the recessed panels as ready-made frames for family photographs, she hangs the door horizontally above the sofa and leaves the crystal doorknob in place as a quirky flourish.

Chapter Five

Embellis

This may go against what your mother told you, but here goes: It's OK to embellish a little—or even a lot. Good design concerns itself with the whole story, and every good story includes embellishments. Your interiors are probably dying for the details, so why not dish them out? The *Trading Spaces* rooms featured in this chapter are about to tell all, so lean in close and learn things that you *should* repeat.

If this card could
love
it would love only you. Until
the end of time, forever and
ever, because you hung the

hments
Worth
Repeating

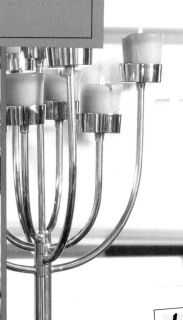

Feathered Nest

1 PRUDENCE PAYS Before giving a piece of furniture the heave-ho, give it a once-over to see if it can be repurposed or revised to suit your scheme. With its fussy decorative elements cut off, this upholstered bed is sleek and sophisticated.

2 LANGUAGE OF LOVE Whether it's a handwritten love letter or a heartfelt card, the written word can be turned into art. The sentiments on this greeting card launched the romantic theme of this room. Adhere a card to a piece of paper and slip it inside a frame for inexpensive artwork.

3 SILVERY SENSATIONS This newly painted nightstand steps out in style, casting aside the notion that stain is for wood and silver is for metal. Chrome spray paint on top, dry-brush silver paint on the body, and shiny new knobs on the drawers give it 1930s Hollywood glitz.

4 SOFT TOUCH Fabrics can coordinate a room in less time than it takes to paint. This sage green fabric backdrop ties in with the green on the ceiling, eliminating the need to repaint that surface. The panels cover the walls, creating a plush backdrop for the bed.

5 PLUCKY PERSONALITY Feathers—lots of them—soften these walls more than wallpaper or a faux paint treatment ever could. The wall itself becomes art.

6 LOUNGE ACT This shapely chaise lounge invites relaxation. Proving that little details mean a lot, the silver-painted feet—formerly finials on the old bedposts—unite the chaise with the other furnishings in the room.

DESIGNED BY **HILDI**

5 ▶

For this bedroom redo, the owners said they were in the mood for almost anything. Hildi is definitely in the mood for love when she embellishes the walls with feathers and creates this soft, sensuous sanctuary.

6 ▼

▼This silvery mirror and chest of drawers recall the glitz of 1930s Art Deco style, as do the sparkling accessories. Roses and candlesticks are musts in any romantic retreat.

before

▶ Nashville: Rosella Court

This generous-size bedroom has plenty of furnishings and even some color on the walls and ceiling. Still, it lacks impact. The furnishings are a matching ensemble of the nothing-special variety. The swag and panels dressing the window are too formal for the room, which has a slight beach-cottage feel. Artwork is lost on the walls, which lead into a tray ceiling. Hildi plans to soften the look of the room with color, fabrics, and a special wall treatment; her goal is a really romantic retreat. The furniture will return, albeit with a new look, but the exercise equipment has to go. "That is the least romantic thing I could imagine," Hildi says.

► Some beds are overdone, with too many pillows, too much pattern, and the standard tired throw draped at the foot. A bit contemporary, this bed is casually elegant. Sheet ensembles, available in many colors, are affordable bed embellishments that can come out from beneath the covers. Fold the top of a sheet over a bedspread to create a band of color and use solid-color pillowcases instead of expensive shams. Your splurge can be a single patterned pillow, such as a long bolster, that breaks up the solids. To learn an easy method for making your own bolster, turn to page 24.

The owners of this bedroom said they didn't want hay on their bedroom walls, a reference to one of Hildi's more memorable treatments. Laying out a few hopeful boundaries (no pink, no florals, no hay), they think they're ready for virtually anything. "We don't care whether we like the room or hate the room when we're done with it," one owner says. "I think this is just going to be a memorable experience, and probably we'll just have a hoot about the whole thing."

Hildi has her own ideas: Hay is passé—it's already been done. Feathers are the latest news. With some 60,000 fluffy plumes—give or take a few—Hildi builds a true love nest. After painting the sage green walls white, the team begins the laborious task of hot-gluing thousands of beige feathers to every wall.

Hildi makes no excuses or apologies for her embellishments, whether they come in the form of feathers, hay, or something else. "They are alternative wall treatments," she says. "I do them so that others can be inspired and carry them out their way, not my way."

The inspiration for the room started with a greeting card; the front of the card features a verse about

◄ When you decide on a color for furnishings, carry it over to the accessories. Painted silver, this lamp and frame create a serene scene on the bedside table. Introducing a new color would have been jarring.

◄This near life-size rendition of Hildi's legs is a subtly sensuous addition to the room. To create a similar wall hanging, use a computer to manipulate a photo to give it an artsy quality, have a copy store print out an oversize image, and then adhere it to a wooden frame.

love. The soft colors and gentle ambience of the room echo the sentiments and look of the card. The room moves to the sensuous side with an angular chaise and a wall hanging featuring shapely bare legs—Hildi's, in fact—in a pose reminiscent of Marilyn Monroe with her skirt aflutter in *The Seven Year Itch*.

"If this room could talk, it would talk about love," Hildi says.

▶When painting furniture, think beyond a flat coat of paint. Increase the impact of your paint projects by experimenting with new techniques. A dry-brush technique gives the lower portion of this dresser depth; chrome spray paint coats the top in solid silver.

Romantic Intentions

Whether your tastes lean toward casual cottage, ornate Victorian, or somewhere in between, follow your heart to bring romantic style to your home.

▶ **Introduce surprises.** Like a love note tucked in a lunch box, little surprises add charm to everyday rooms. Drape mirrors, wall sconces, and chandeliers with crystals or strings of pearls. Adhere fringe to the bottom of a lampshade for a flirty flourish. Scented candles and flowers, especially roses, are always welcome additions in a romantic retreat.

▶ **Lighten up.** If you're not quite ready for Valentine's red, spark romance with a light palette, such as creamy whites or pastels with a mere hint of color. Choose furnishings that have an airy quality, such as a glass-top table or a metal bed. Relax formal pieces by painting them white. Add sparkle to plain furnishings with a coat of silver paint.

▶ **Strike a balance.** To prevent a romantically styled room from becoming strictly a woman's domain, bring in masculine touches. A mahogany writing table or a cushioned bench can anchor a group of white furnishings. Instead of a big bouquet of flowers in a glass vase, fill an urn with greenery or pheasant feathers.

▶ **Mix it up.** Love knows no boundaries, so go ahead and mix countries and periods, antiques and reproductions—even flea market finds. Look for subtle similarities, such as graceful curves, to pull the look together. Or unify disparate pieces by painting them the same color.

▲Almost anyone—even a child—can weave fabric strips around a wire frame to create this charming lampshade. If you can't find a bare wire frame in the desired shape and size, purchase one that's already covered and remove the fabric or paper.

Rags to Riches Lampshade

Create a fabulous lampshade with colorful fabric strips woven over a wire frame.

Tear all fabrics into ¾- to 1-inch-wide strips (snip the fabric to start the tears, if needed) and roll into a ball. Tie one end of a gingham strip to one end of the shade frame near a vertical support. Wrap the fabric up and over the top, continuing back down the inside of the frame (A). Continue wrapping around the frame, hand-stitching lengths of

▶ **MATERIALS**
Wire frame for lampshade
1 to 2 yards red and white cotton gingham fabric
¼ to ½ yard each of several other red and white cotton prints
Coordinating thread

▶ **TOOLS**
Scissors
Sewing needle
Tapestry or upholstery needle (optional, for weaving)

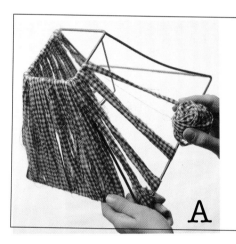

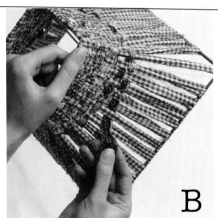

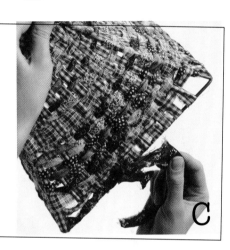

A   B   C

The Alternate Route... If a material is flexible, you may be able to use it to create a woven shade. However, do not use flammable materials. If in doubt do not leave a lit lamp unattended. Here are a few alternative materials to use to cover a shade.

▶ **RIBBON** For a crisper appearance, weave ribbon, braiding, or cord onto a wire frame as shown.

▶ **PAPER** Use heavier paper stock cut into long strips; at the starting points, fold over one end and hot-glue. Weave as instructed. To add paper strips, hide loose ends inside the shade and trim after weaving.

▶ **FLASHING** Wearing protective gloves, use tin snips to cut metal strips. Fold flashing end over the wire frame and clamp with pliers to hold the end in place. Space weaving to allow light to filter through the lampshade.

fabric to the strip as necessary. Keep the strips taut, not tight, on the frame. Tie off or stitch the end of the final strip next to the starting point.

Select a red and white print for weaving. Tie or sew one end of a strip near the original starting point on the shade. Thread the other end of the fabric strip through an upholstery or tapestry needle, if desired. (You can also use fingertips, as shown, to weave the strips.) Weave the fabric strips over and under the gingham warp, taking care to catch both front (outside) and back (inside) strips

(B). Weave all around the shade, alternating "overs and unders" from row to row and adding strips of fabric as needed. Use your fingers to pack strips toward the starting row; this will help tighten the weave.

Sew or tie off the end of the final strip; trim excess fabric.

To finish the shade, tie a strip at the bottom (C); thread a needle onto the other end, if desired. Wrap the strip around the wire by inserting the fabric between the gingham warp strips and pulling to cover any exposed wire. Repeat at the top of the shade, if needed.

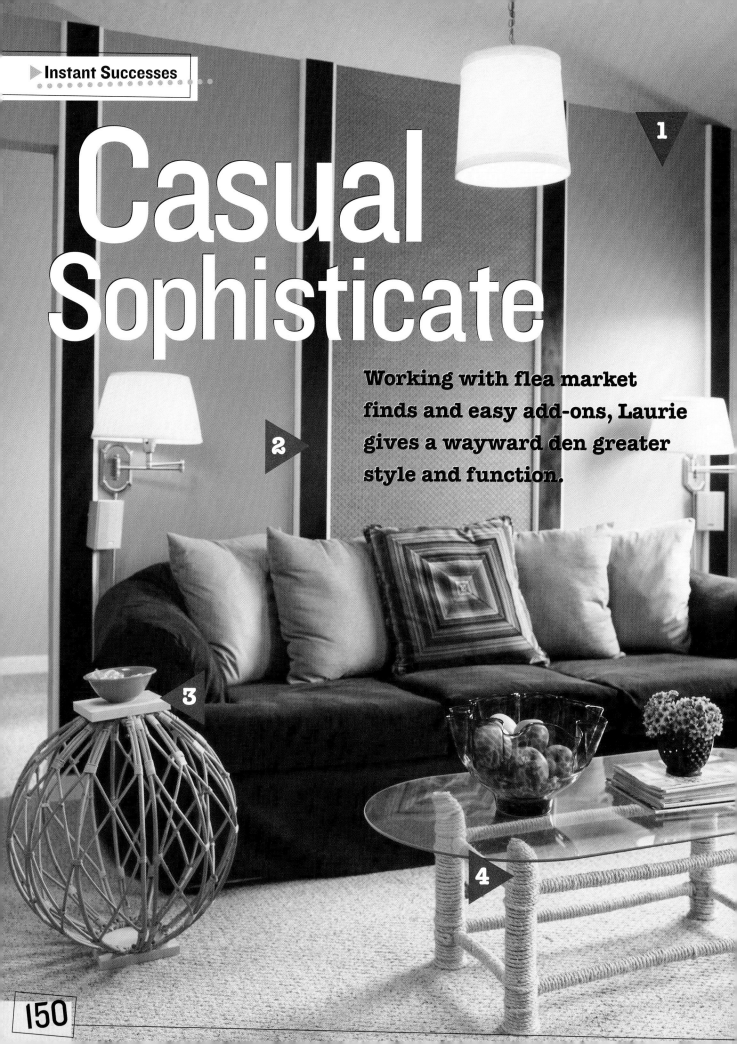

Casual Sophisticate

Working with flea market finds and easy add-ons, Laurie gives a wayward den greater style and function.

1

2

3

4

1 THE GREAT DIVIDE Adding this wall creates space for an exercise area on one end of the room and keeps the treadmill out of view. The wall stops where the ceiling begins to rise, keeping the reconfigured spaces open and airy.

2 MOLDING AN IMAGE Walls can be a visual treat all by themselves. Chocolate brown molding and white quarter round add interesting dimension, contrast, and architectural detail to this flat surface. The wide orange stripe is a sisal-like panel applied like wallpaper over the blue-painted wall. The varied widths of the stripes add visual rhythm.

3 BRIGHT IDEA With an open mind and a bit of imagination, Laurie turns a seemingly useless castoff into a beautiful addition. Two wood squares transform this light fixture into a sculptural end table that is easy to move around the room.

4 IT'S A WRAP Too brassy can be too tacky. Sisal rope tones down shiny legs on the coffee table, contributing natural texture that fits the casual style of the room.

5 INSPIRATION STARTING POINT Every room needs a place to begin. Laurie says this fabric inspired the fresh color palette and the striped treatment on the new wall.

6 UPWARD MOBILITY Give a room the illusion of height by taking window treatments to the ceiling. This den has a high-pitched ceiling; hanging the blinds high on the wall gives the window a sense of grandeur and makes the ceiling seem even higher. It also balances the 8-foot-tall wall, creating an even visual plane.

DESIGNED BY **LAURIE**

etting their trepidation show a wee bit, the owners of this den say they have "a Plan B" if they don't like their room when it's done. New furniture is on hold, and paint colors have been chosen. "But we anticipate liking it," one owner quickly adds.

Laurie's Plan A is an ingenious mix of new and old. The new includes an 8-foot-tall wall that creates two areas within the larger space: a nook that hides a treadmill and a main space for relaxing and watching TV. The already ambitious wall project could have been a nondescript surface to back a sofa against. Under Laurie's direction, however, it becomes an artful presence with multicolor, multiwidth stripes. After painting the wall ice blue—a fresh partner of the chocolate brown in some of the fabrics and trims—Laurie applies a synthetic sisal-like panel in an orange hue, creating the look of wide stripes.

▶before

▶Nashville: Murphywood Crossing

This den is a decent size and has a high ceiling that adds to the feeling of spaciousness. The furnishings are fairly formal; however, a large treadmill takes up one corner. Is this an exercise/rec room or a sophisticated getaway? Laurie plans to answer the question by adding an 8-foot-tall wall that will create a nook for the treadmill on one side and a stylish place for relaxing on the other. She wants to refresh the furnishings with some easy embellishments and flea market finds. The yellow walls will remain; the ceiling and new wall will get fresh paint.

◄Custom artwork and fine furniture can be affordable for do-it-yourselfers. This abstract collage is made of construction paper that was cut into random shapes and then layered and decoupaged. The lamp base is embellished with rope, and the table base is made from two oversize candlesticks. The glass top was salvaged from the owners' existing end table.

▼At $54 a yard, this striped fabric was a splurge. The indulgence was worth it, though, considering the fact that the fabric inspired the overall look of the room. "Finding that set a certain color palette and mood for the room that is just so fresh and now," Laurie says. The fabric appears on two chairs and pillows.

◄A decorative folding screen is a conventional way to hide unsightly exercise equipment. Laurie went beyond conventional by having Amy Wynn build a real wall out of drywall. The wall turns the spacious den into a two-part room with clear functions—one area for relaxing and one for working out.

▼Paint isn't the only way to change an undesirable finish. Sisal rope covers the brassy legs on this coffee table, complementing the rope-wrapping on a nearby table lamp. Curtain rods, chandeliers, and lampshades are other candidates for this easy embellishment. Use a hot-glue gun to adhere rope, a string of beads, a feather boa, or garland. If possible, grab a partner so one person can glue while the other wraps.

Molding attached vertically to the wall forms three-dimensional stripes that frame the wide panels and add architectural interest.

The old takes many forms, all with a common denominator: fresh style at a low cost. In fact, several items are doctored flea market finds repurposed into functional pieces. Two beefy wooden candlesticks stack up as the base for a side table. A bamboo globe-shape light fixture is repurposed into an end table. Sisal rope wraps around the legs of a coffee table and the base of a lamp to add texture and casual style. And the ceiling is freshened with what Laurie calls "5 gallons of oops"—mis-mixed

paint she purchased from a home center for a fraction of the regular cost. Though it doesn't perfectly match the existing yellow on the walls, the subtle color variation remains a secret, thanks to shadows and the height of the ceiling.

Laurie is enthusiastic about this multifunctional, create-something-from-nothing space. "I love this room! I love this room!" she says.

The homeowners, while apprehensive at first, quickly grow to love the room too. When Paige guides the owners through the doorway to the casually elegant main area, any thoughts of activating Plan B are quickly squelched. "This is beautiful," one owner says. "I absolutely love this."

Recycled Style

Having a limited decorating budget can actually help you create conversation-starting style. Some of the most interesting finds are lurking in antiques stores and flea markets that are off the beaten path. Keep these tips in mind for savvy scavenging:

▸ **Embellish and adorn.** Scatter little surprises throughout a room. A vintage brooch pinned to a pillow adds charm. Billiard balls drilled with holes and fitted with screws become fun drawer pulls.

▸ **Refresh and renew.** Look beyond nicks and imperfections to focus on shape. Paint can cover most flaws; it takes carpentry skills to change furniture curves and lines. If purchasing a chair, sofa, or bench, keep comfort in mind too. Painting a chair or adding a slipcover to a sofa may make it look better, but it won't add any comfort.

▸ **Reinvent and reinterpret.** Creative thinking gives a room unexpected visual interest. An old wooden ironing board can morph into a sofa table. Give a drum a new beat as a nightstand or an end table. With a do-it-yourself wiring kit, a silver coffeepot or gallon jug can be transformed into a table lamp.

◂This shapely table bends the design rule of "Form follows function." Two small wooden squares level the former light fixture, transforming it into an end table. With the tiny tabletop, it's more decorative than functional, though it will hold a small snack.

▲Personalize a plain mirror with an elegant monogram flanked by stenciled designs, such as these leaves and berries. Use purchased stencils or make your own.

Elegant Monogrammed Mirror

Etching cream lets you permanently make your mark on the mirror of your choice.

▸ **MATERIALS**
Clear adhesive-back vinyl
Computer printout of desired letter and designs (or use purchased stencils)
Mirror
Etching cream (available at crafts and art supply stores)

▸ **TOOLS**
Pen
Crafts knife
Paper punch
Latex gloves
Foam brush or artist's brush
Clean lint-free rag

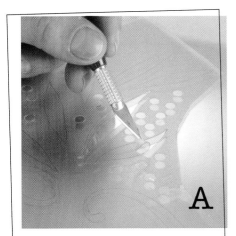

A

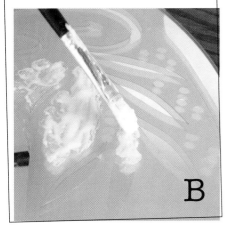

B

Trace a letter onto vinyl (leave the backing on). Stencil designs on each side of the letter, following the shape of the mirror.

Cut away excess vinyl from around the sketched designs, leaving enough space for the berries, if desired; use a paper punch to create the round berry shapes.

Pull away a small portion of the backing and position the vinyl design on the mirror. Continue to pull away the backing paper, adhering the vinyl to the glass and working out any bubbles.

Use a crafts knife to cut the design outlines (A). Remove the vinyl only in areas where you want to apply the etching cream.

Wear latex gloves for protection and apply etching cream to the cutaway areas, using a foam brush or artist's brush (B) and following the manufacturer's directions. Cover exposed glass with additional vinyl. Stir cream thoroughly before use and apply evenly and thickly, allowing the cream to set for the prescribed time or longer. Rinse away the cream with water, remove the vinyl, and polish the glass with a clean lint-free rag.

Tips for Success

▸ Clean the glass surface before you begin.

▸ Work in a well-ventilated area. Wear latex gloves and goggles to protect yourself from the caustic cream.

▸ If desired, transfer another design to the adhesive-back vinyl. Place a piece of carbon paper on top of the vinyl and layer the desired motif on top of that. (The motif can be on a piece of fabric or wrapping paper or sketched on another piece of paper.) Trace over the outline of the motif or pattern with a pencil, pressing to transfer the design to the vinyl below. Lift off the pattern and carbon paper to reveal the transferred design.

DESIGNED BY **RICK**

1 SHEER DELIGHT Painted orange and wrapped in sheer fabric, this chandelier turns out the lights on its serious side. The unconventional treatment is a nod to the Caribbean, where mosquito netting around light sources and beds is common.

2 ALL RIGHT IN WHITE Paint works wonders on almost any surface, so think beyond walls and wood furnishings. Treated with a fresh coat of white paint, these blinds have staying power in the island-inspired scheme. A paint sprayer makes quick work of the potentially time-consuming paint job.

3 STYLISH SEATING Matched dining sets may be a safe way to go for the timid, yet they seem almost criminal in a carefree setting. This blue bench brings personality to the room and playful contrast to the more serious wood pieces.

4 WINGING IT Mimic the look of carved wood or add ornamental detailing to a plain furnishing without busting the budget. This bench takes flight with wooden biscuits painted yellow, orange, and blue and formed into butterflies.

5 INSIDE OUT Many items intended for use outdoors look equally good when placed inside. These shutters, distressed for a weathered

appearance, are more than mere decoration: They play a functional role by balancing the oddly proportioned window with another.

6 TOP IT OFF Crown molding adds finesse to any room. Here, new molding painted white draws the eye up to lighter colors and airy space.

7 SPACE ENHANCER Mirrors make small rooms seem larger by bouncing light around the space. This mirror maximizes natural light from windows on both the opposite and the adjacent wall. Mirrors can also double as artwork when they have interesting frames.

Colorfully
Caribbean

The owners of this dining room live far from sugary beaches and azure waters, so Rick gives them an in-home island-inspired getaway by bringing in lively color and room-refreshing accents.

Aside from their ability to wield a paintbrush, the owners of this home readily admit that their aptitude for interior design is limited to signing checks for hired contractors. The random squares they painted on the upper walls of their dining room get an A for effort, but the color, scale, and balance in the room need improvement.

Rick jumps right in with a plan to remedy the wrongs. His energetic agenda calls for infusing the room with color and transporting it to the Tropics. Rick is sure the design will appeal to at least one of the owners, who's a native of Barbados. "You don't come from a place with all of these colors and not have it in your life," Rick says.

One of the first things to go is the painted squares, which did little to bring cheer into the room. After sanding them away—an extra layer or two of paint can form a noticeable ledge—Rick splashes the walls and ceiling in sunshine yellow. With the standard-issue chair rail removed, the yellow travels freely down the wall before meeting up with an orange that veers toward terra-cotta. Stippling brings depth to the lower walls—a big payoff for a minimal investment of time and effort.

The wood-tone blinds that gave the room a dark, denlike feel freshen up with white paint. And now that the team is rolling, nothing is off-limits in this painterly paradise. "We're about to kill the chandelier," Rick forewarns as he dips a brush into the orange paint. In what Paige believes is a *Trading Spaces* first, the chandelier is soon awash in color—glass crystals, dangling beads, and all.

The happy-go-lucky yellow and orange join up with an energized blue on the furnishings and accents. Two shades of blue and crackle medium give four shutters designed for outdoor use weathered good looks. Hung

◄This table setting is a relaxed mix of casual linens, flowers, and dishes. Mimicking tiki torches, candles circle around the table runner. The multicolor mix of plates engages the eye. For fun-loving fetes, vintage or new Fiestaware will always serve up style, regardless of what's on the menu.

▼Putting lively colors together actually helps offset their intensity. Repeating the colors in different ways, such as using the yellow and orange for the butterflies on the bench, unifies a room. And as these walls show, you don't need a chair rail or wallpaper border for a two-tone treatment.

►Pennsylvania: Madison Circle

Dark green lower walls, a heavy area rug, and wood-tone blinds and furnishings are weighing down this small dining room. The stained chair rail visually drags the room down even further, and the mismatched windows make the room seem off balance. The fussy chandelier doesn't fit the style of the room by any stretch of the imagination. Rick plans a clean sweep of the cramped quarters so he can create a "Caribbean Colonial" theme featuring lively colors and fun embellishments.

▼Conventional wisdom says it's best to center a table in a dining room. This table and dining room are an exception to the rule. The room is small and the table is big. Positioning the table toward a far wall allows better flow in the room and prevents the table from dominating the space.

▶Orange paint and new lampshades relax this formal chandelier. (Conversely, beads and baubles that may be as close as your jewelry box are fast fix-ups for plain fixtures.) The sheer fabric swaddling this fixture is purely decorative; in the Tropics, though, it would keep bugs from swarming to the lights.

◀Slipcovers tend to fall in the "love 'em or hate 'em" category. These tailored skirts may give naysayers something to think about. They leave the slatted chair backs exposed to tie in with the bench, and the casual solid and striped fabrics relax the Mission-style pieces.

at the sides of each window, the shutters take the room "totally into the tropical," Rick says. Their presence does more than evoke a mood: The shutters help balance the oddly proportioned windows, giving the illusion that they are the same size.

Rick's pièce de résistance was a bit slow in coming. A custom-designed bench inspired by carved Caribbean folk art kept Ty whittling away for hours. The holdup had nothing to do with actual carving but rather with the time-consuming process of joining the slats and adhering the wooden biscuits that are cleverly formed into butterfly shapes. Painted bright blue and tucked under the short window, the bench has a starring role in the extroverted room. It also casually mixes with the more formal wood tones of the table and chairs. The chairs wear floor-skimming skirts in fabrics that pull in all the colors of the room.

In a final flourish, Rick swathes the chandelier in sheer fabric. Questioned by his team, Rick says, "There's logic behind it. It's something that's done in the Tropics, in the Caribbean." Happily, mosquitoes

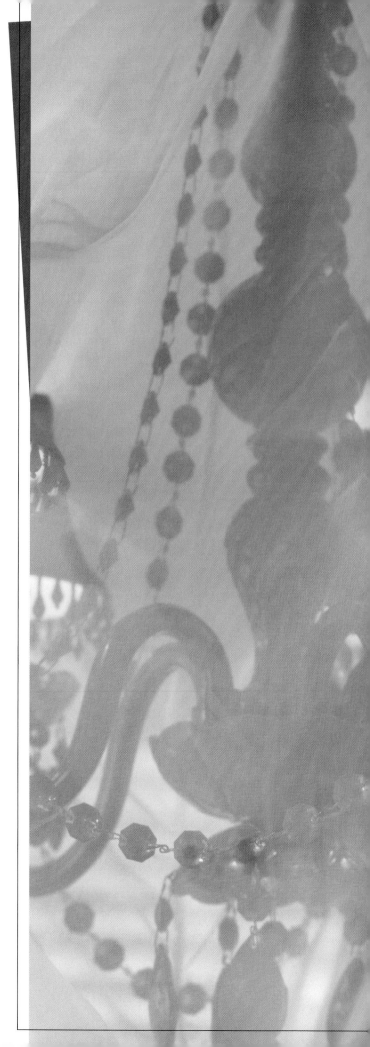

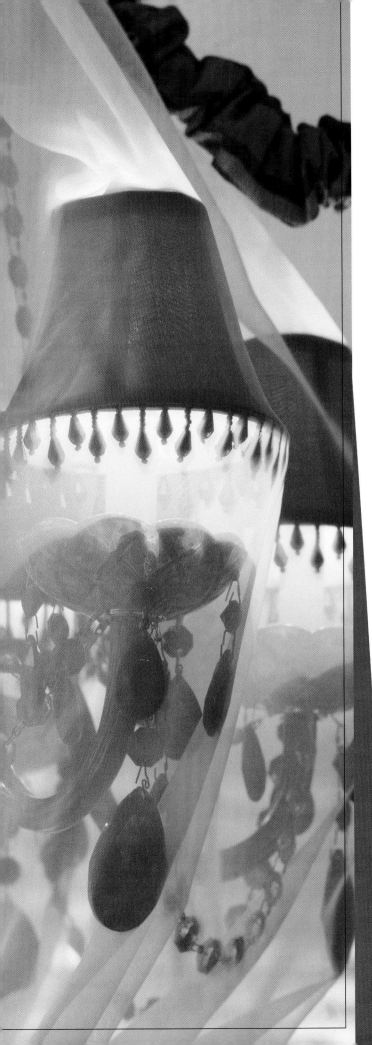

won't be visiting this indoor island, so the fabric remains purely decorative.

The chandelier treatment isn't an issue with the owners, who are swept away by the carefree color and newfound sense of scale and balance in the room. "Wow!" exclaims one owner. "This is awesome!"

Dressed-Down Dining

f your tastes lean more toward takeout than fine dining, take your formal dining room down a notch by forgoing fussiness.

▶ **Mix things up.** Quit saving for that table and chair ensemble. Your "matched set" can be a group of outdoor wicker chairs teamed with a well-worn farm table. Even one unmatched chair at the end of a table breaks up typical uniformity. Mixing stained and painted wood finishes also sets an informal tone.

▶ **Bring in textures.** By their very nature, rough textures have a casual quality. Wicker, rattan, pine, and iron, for example, are less formal than polished woods and glass. Factor in texture when choosing any design element, from furnishings to fabrics.

▶ **Say it with slipcovers.** Slipcovers are an easy way to dramatically alter the look and feel of a room. Skip the flowing, fussy silks and brocades for more-tailored slipcovers in easy-care cottons. Choose fun colors, lively patterns, or interesting textures. A plain skirt or a fabric "cozy" that slips over a chair back will provide a sleeker look. For another easy option, pop colorful cushions on the seats.

▶ **Paint it pretty.** It's OK to paint fine furniture! Paint can temper the formality of a piece and engage the eye. Add extra dimension with antiquing medium, crackle medium, or glaze. Or rub off some of the paint before it dries or sand off dried paint in areas that would naturally get the most wear, such as corners and around drawer handles.

▶ **Set the table.** Keep the tablecloth in storage for Thanksgiving. In a casual dining room, place mats and a table runner will serve the daily fare. Choose casual, coarse weaves, easy-care cottons, and wrinkle-resistant fabrics. Colorful everyday dishes can take the place of china; mixing colors and patterns will relax the look even more.

Superfast Snapshot Valance

String happy memories and other favorite photos across a sunny window and you'll always enjoy the view.

Scan favorite photographs into a computer and use imaging software to convert the prints to black and white or copy color snapshots in black and white using a photocopy machine.

Print 4×6-inch black and white copies onto 8×10-inch gloss photo paper and trim to include a 2-inch-wide border around each photo.

Use a laminating machine or take the prints to a photocopy store or office supply store to have them centered in 10mm laminating plastic (A).

After laminating, evenly space small grommets across the top of each laminated image (B). (Space the grommets ⁵⁄₁₆ inch from the top and 2 inches from the sides.)

Secure a wire at the top of the window frame (or stretch a wire from wall to wall) and hang the laminated photos along the wire using #40 S hooks (C).

◄ Black and white architectural photography—views captured on vacation—gives this valance a theme. Choose any subject that suits your mood, such as photos of relatives or favorite toys for a child's room, or fruit and veggies for a kitchen sink window. Have fun with the possibilities!

A

B

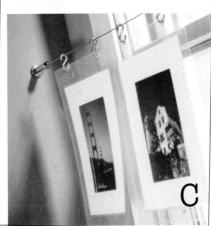

C

▶ MATERIALS
Assorted photographs

Gloss photo paper (8×10 inches)

Small grommets

Wire

Hardware, such as eye screws, to secure wire to window frame

#40 S hooks

▶ TOOLS
Computer, scanner, and photo-quality printer, or a photocopy machine (or access to a photocopy store)

Tape measure

Paper cutter or scissors

Laminating machine (or access to a photocopy or office supply store)

Grommet tool

The Alternate Route
Laminating works for lots of different decorative items that can hang as a valance. Consider these alternatives for color and fun:

▶ Fabric swatches

▶ Children's drawings

▶ Leaves

▶ Art paper

▶ Decorative embroidery medallions (available at fabric or crafts stores)

▶ Postcards

Embellish the Facts

Armed with adhesives and assorted embellishments, the *Trading Spaces* designers give plain fabrics, pillows, walls, and lampshades (to name but a few surfaces) style and character. So can you!

Beauty by the Yard

You're on a roll when you find a decorative feature you love on, well, a roll. Buy the affordable embellishments *below* by the yard and use them to dress up all kinds of decorative features, including furniture, frames, lampshades, linens, and shelves.

1) **Decorative cording.** This decorating staple comes in many thicknesses, colors, and color combinations.

2) **Beads on a string.** Pearls, silver or gold balls, and glittery plastic orbs are some of the many options.

3) **Beaded ribbon.** Already threaded onto a tightly woven fabric strip, these beads are ideal for edging a lampshade or plain shelf.

4) **Ribbon.** Varieties with wired edges (like the one shown) hold their shape—use these to make bows for a basket or mirror. Nonwired versions are perfect for embellishing fabrics, such as pillow covers and sheets.

5) **Fringe.** Like cording, fringe comes in various thicknesses, lengths, and colors. Use a substantial fringe like this one to trim an ottoman or a slipcovered chair.

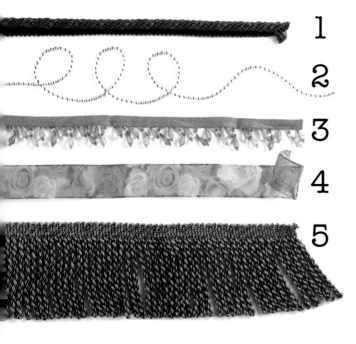

Little Bits

Tiny treasures await discovery in every crafts and fabric store. These are only a few possibilities:

A. Buttons. Garage sales, Grandma's attic, and antiques stores all can yield some fabulous button finds. Buttons add a note of fun to lots of surfaces. Frame a family photo in a colorful variety or stitch a vintage button collection to a pillow.

B. Tassels galore. Whether you hang them from the knobs of an armoire or tack them to the corners of the dining table, tassels add color and flair.

C. Lovely leaves. These delicate leaves can soften the look of matting or a lampshade.

D. Paper flowers. A dab of glue is all it takes to position these flowers on a picture frame—or anywhere you like.

E. Bountiful beads. Add color and dimension to surfaces with beads of all kinds.

Make It Stick

All the decorative items available in the design universe may be outnumbered by the adhesive products designed to support them! Stroll the adhesives aisle at crafts, fabric, and hobby stores and at home centers to see the amazing variety. Always read the label on the package to find out if you're buying the right adhesive for the job.

White glue is a good all-around adhesive for bonding lightweight embellishments to surfaces, such as tiny beads or sparkles to a lampshade.

Spray adhesive adheres paper to paper. Use it in a well-ventilated area and protect surrounding surfaces from overspray.

Hook-and-loop tape is handy because it lets you easily remove the secured item whenever you want. It comes in a variety of sizes, types, and strengths. Adhesive-back and sew-on tapes are available.

Polyurethane-base glues bond virtually any material and are waterproof.

Permanent fabric adhesive secures fabric to fabric. It works best with lightweight materials.

Fast-drying, superstrong glue comes in a handy tiny tube. Keep one in a desk drawer for making fast repairs and to secure all kinds of objects to different materials.

Embellishing adhesive is an acid-free, water-soluble adhesive that dries to a clear, repositionable, tacky surface. It's ideal for applying gilt, dry pigments, embossing powders, and paper.

Clear glue sticks are available in acid-free formulations for adhering photos to surfaces. This adhesive dries fast and is nontoxic, so it's safe for children to use.

Jewelry adhesive can be used to attach beads, stones, sequins, decorative plastic, and other items to almost any surface. It provides a clear, waterproof bond.

Glue guns and glue sticks are hot items for your decorating holster. Hot-melt guns heat up to more than 350°F and offer a secure bond between surfaces that can stand up to the high temperature, such as wood. Low-temperature glue guns heat up to 200°F—cooler than hot-melt guns and easier on your fingers. They're an ideal choice for joining materials that could melt or burn when exposed to high temperatures, such as foam or paper.

Embellish with Stamps and Stencils

If you don't have a flair for freehand painting, use stencils and stamps to create charming painted designs on fabric, walls, furniture, and more.

Stamp-On Style

Choose foam stamps that suit the look you want to achieve; if you can't find exactly what you are looking for, make a stamp of your own design following the instructions in "Tips for Success" on page 171. If you use cosmetic sponges or a small artist's brush to apply paint to your stamp, you'll be able to use various colors on appropriate parts of the stamp. Otherwise, use a small foam roller to evenly cover a stamp with one paint color.

1) **Start with a foam stamp** and acrylic paint. You'll also need cosmetic sponges, a foam roller, or an artist's brush to apply the paint color(s) to the stamp. Apply a base coat of color to the wall or other surface; let dry.

2) **Pour paint onto a paper plate.** Using the desired applicator, apply an even layer of acrylic paint onto the raised design of the stamp (A).

3) **Press the stamp onto the wall,** using even pressure (B). Carefully lift the stamp from the wall.

4) **Continue stamping the surface.** Stamp at regular intervals for a border or stamp randomly for a more informal look.

5) **When you have finished stamping,** use an artist's brush to touch up any unevenly stamped designs.

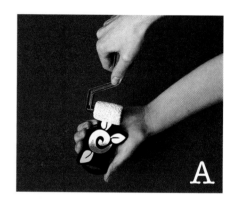

A

B

Style from the Aisles

Special foam stamps—which are larger and easier to hold than smaller rubber stamps used for various paper crafts—make embellishing walls and other paintable surfaces quick and easy. Foam stamps are available at crafts stores in nearly every motif imaginable. Small tubes of acrylic crafts paint are economical for stamping; cosmetic sponges are great paint applicators.

◄Stencils of many sizes and motifs are available at crafts stores. Use them to embellish all kinds of surfaces—from pillows and sheets to lampshades and tabletops. Specially formulated stencil crayons, creams, and even acrylic paints can be used with stencils.

Make a Statement with Stencils

Embellishing with stencils is an easy process. To paint on fabric, follow these steps:

1) Wash the fabric in plain water first. (Residues from detergent or fabric softener may prevent paint from adhering.) Dry the fabric; iron.

2) Mix acrylic paint with textile medium. Use the ratio listed on the bottle of textile medium.

3) Lay the fabric taut on a plastic-covered surface; secure with tape. If you stencil onto a double thickness of fabric, such as a pillowcase, position a piece of cardboard or poster board (cut to size) between the fabric layers to prevent the paint from bleeding through to the bottom layer.

4) Position the stencil on the fabric. Apply the paint mixture to the fabric with a stenciling brush, using a dabbing motion. Set the fabric as directed on the textile medium bottle to ensure permanency and washability.

NOTE: To stencil embellishments on walls or lampshades, use acrylic paint without adding textile medium. Or use stencil crayons or stencil cream. When applying stencils to walls, use stencil adhesive spray or low-tack painter's tape to secure the stencil in place. If you plan to switch colors from stencil to stencil, use a different stenciling brush for each color.

▲Basic stenciling in one color—using a single-layer stencil as shown here—is by far the easiest method; stenciling becomes more difficult as you incorporate additional colors and use multilayered stencils.

Tips for Success

▶ If you can't find the stamp motifs you want for your particular project, make your own. Trace a design onto an old computer mouse pad or a sheet of flat sponge. Cut out the design with scissors or a crafts knife. To use the mouse pad stamp, roll paint onto it with a small foam roller and apply to the desired surface. To use the sponge stamp, dampen it with water so it expands. Wring out as much water as possible before applying paint and stamping.

▶ Dipping a stamp directly into paint often results in the stamp becoming saturated; a saturated stamp produces uneven, unsatisfactory results. To avoid problems, use a foam roller or cosmetic sponges to apply paint to the raised design of the stamp.

Embellish for Style

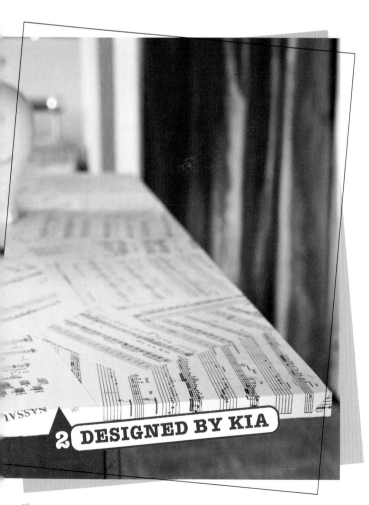

1 **DESIGNED BY LAURIE**

2 **DESIGNED BY KIA**

3 **DESIGNED BY CHRISTI**

Trading Spaces designers cannot tell a lie: They love to embellish! Here are some ways they've perked up plain furnishings.

1 TRANSFORM A TABLE An ordinary white table becomes the centerpiece of this dining room in Austin: Wyoming Valley Drive when Laurie wields paint and fabric in creative ways. The floor-length skirt instills a more formal look, yet because it doesn't cover the top of the table, it need not be washed after every meal. (Securing the skirt with hook-and-loop tape makes it easy to remove when necessary.) The design on the fabric inspired the octagon- and diamond-shape stencils added to the tabletop.

2 TUNE UP A COUNTERTOP Decoupage—the art of applying decorative paper images to a flat surface—is an easy way to embellish something ordinary. In Philadelphia: Cresheim Road, Kia applies sheet music to a kitchen countertop belonging to a musically inclined couple. Nontoxic sealer protects the images from wear.

3 ALL THE TRIMMINGS Christi employs at least two creative embellishment techniques in this bedroom featured in Minnesota: Pleasure Creek Circle. A pair of plain purchased lampshades, for example, takes on a playful air when decorative feather trim is hot-glued around the rims. The walls gain new perspective near the ceiling with the addition of a three-dimensional border created with joint compound and a stencil.

4 EARN FRINGE BENEFITS An existing sofa, table, or chair can take on new personality when you add decorative cording or fringe. (A hot-glue gun generally works best to secure the embellishment in place. If you use a staple gun, plan to hide the staples with something decorative, such as cording, hot-glued in place.) In Minneapolis: 11th Avenue, the sofa looks great, so Gen skips a slipcover and instead glues on this lush, long black fringe near the bottom.

5 HANG A GARDEN In San Diego: Duenda Road, Vern plots a hanging garden on a square of dark green paint backed with a field of light green. Clear glass vases, designed to hang on the wall, hold water and a single stem each to bring elegance and color to a formerly ho-hum surface.

5 DESIGNED BY VERN

4 DESIGNED BY GENEVIEVE

TRADING SPACES INSTANT IMPACT

Use the following index as your handy guide to locating the topics, tools, looks, styles, and designers you're looking for. Jump in!

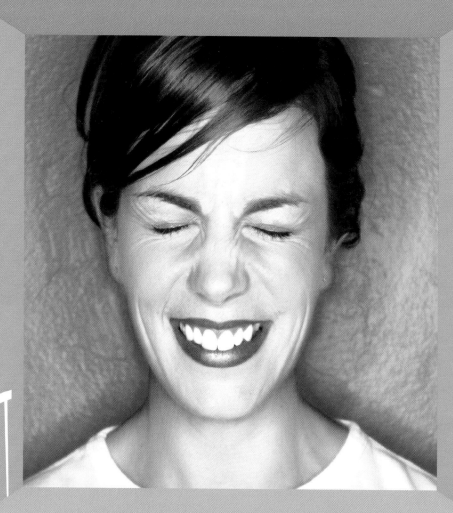

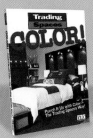